GW01057411

How to Write a Mystery Novel
Behind the Scenes: Creation of a Crime Series

By Gene Grossman,
Author of the popular 15-book
Peter Sharp Legal Mysteries

Magic Lamp Press ™

www.LegalMystery.com

ISBN: 9781450557900

CONTENTS

INTRODUCTION

If you noticed how this book's cover described me, you know that I've written a 'popular' 15-book series mysteries, and the main reason that description is accurate is because of Amazon.com's three divisions, handling print books, ebooks and audiobooks.

Don't be misled: this book is not intended as a commercial for Amazon.com, because there are several other sources for writers to gain popularity that I'll go into later in this book, but at the time I wrote my mysteries, they were the only game in town for getting titles distributed in those three formats without going through an agent or major publishing house.

Of course the landscape continues to change rapidly, and ebooks have finally become mainstream, through the efforts of Amazon's **Kindle**, Barnes & Noble's **Nook**, Sony's **eReader**, Plastic Logic's **Que**, Apple's **iPad**, Borders' **Kobo**, Hearst's **Skiff** [my books are available on all of them], plus all the other devices that are continually coming to market. A generation from now, kids graduating high school may have the same expression on their faces when you mention printed books that kids graduating high school presently have when you mention Johnny Carson. It's called the 'that's before my time' look.

I'm pleasantly surprised by the popularity of my fictional titles, because even while writing them I felt it was taking a big chance... and this thought is being confirmed now, because I've also written 19 non-fiction titles and amazingly, the best-seller of them all is a non-fiction book I completed in 2009 that compromises 24% of my eBook royalties (including all 15 of the **Peter Sharp Legal Mysteries**) – and don't ask why, because I've been trying to figure it out for some time now. The non-fiction title I'm talking about is **Celestial Navigation for the Complete Idiot**, and when writing it I kept thinking to myself "Nobody will want this book, but I don't care if it sells or not, because I'm having a good time explaining it to sailors like me who are interested in the subject..." and that's not a bad attitude to assume when writing a non-fiction title, because your psychological mindset comes through in the writing: the readers can sense that you really care about them learning the subject you're writing about – and they appreciate it.

It might also interest you to know that the book you're now reading is running a close second to the Celestial Navigation title, which means that if you have choice of which to write, I'd suggest non-fiction. However, since the reason you're reading this book is because you've probably already got your heart set on writing a mystery or detective novel, you might as well get it out of your system before switching over to non-fiction.

Chapter One: GETTING STARTED

If you plan on being a one-trick pony, then any type of character you want to create will probably be just fine, as long as you do a good job at it. But, if you plan on writing a series of books featuring the same protagonist (leading character), then you'd better spend some time crafting him (or her), because the character traits your main protagonist starts out with will have to carry all the future books too, without much of a character arc.

Arthur Conan Doyle wrote 60 stories featuring *Sherlock Holmes* (4 novels + 56 short stories – I know, because I read all of them every five years or so); Agatha Christie had her *Miss Marple* and *Hercule Poirot*; Rex Stout wrote 72 books featuring his armchair detective *Nero Wolfe*, and other authors have created main characters that were successfully brought back time and again.

Ever since reading Edgar Allen Poe's **The Gold Bug** and **Murders in the Rue Morgue** (while in elementary school) and then graduating to Doyle, Stout and Christie, I was hooked on mysteries, so there was never any doubt in my mind that someday I'd write a series of books that featured a main protagonist who could be brought back again for subsequent adventures. The main problem is creating a lead character that deserves to be brought back... and repetition can be a good thing.

You can tell what's working and what's not, the same way you can tell if a movie or television show is working: if you look at your watch more than once during the presentation, it's not working, but if at the end, you're sorry it's over and are looking forward to the next episode or sequel, it's definitely working.

When starting to write the Peter Sharp Legal Mystery series, I wanted to make sure that my protagonist wasn't too perfect. I wanted someone slightly flawed so that the readers could identify with him.

It was bad enough that he's a lawyer, because in a lot of people's minds members of the legal profession rank down at the bottom of the popularity list, about even in the 'trustworthy' category as used car dealers or fast-talking politicians.

The problem is, once you've got a flawed character, you have to figure out some way to overcome the flaws. A blind person can have a seeing-eye-dog. A person in a wheelchair (remember Raymond Burr's ***Ironside***?) has helpers. Someone who doesn't want to leave his house (Nero Wolfe, the original 'armchair detective) can have a 'leg-man' who runs around and does all the footwork for him.

In my case, I decided to make my lead character not exactly the smartest bulb in the lamp. This would require the introduction of another co-star to carry the intellectual burden and accomplish two things:

First, it would create a second banana to the lead character, with admirable traits that exceed those of the main protagonist; and,

Second, it would offer up another character with a distinct personality, who could be a good subject for 'cutting away' from the main plot occasionally, offering a way to manipulate the timeline of the main story.

Once the decision is made to add a co-protagonist, you must be careful to make that person quite different from your lead character, with talents that fill in for the lead character's flaws. My thinking on this matter brought to mind the old thought that 'everyone likes cute kids and dogs,' so what the heck – I threw in one of each.

The dog was easy, because I've always gotten a kick out of that campy painting of Dogs Playing Poker, and I always dreamed of having a Saint Bernard – so, because an author doesn't have to worry about feeding and cleaning up after a fictional pet, a Saint Bernard got the job.

Just having a dog isn't enough: you have to also find what professional actors describe as the secret to getting 'into a character:' you have to find 'a way in.'

In my books, the dog's 'way in' was as the pet of my lead character's co-star – the other half of the proposition – a cute kid... but not just any 'cute kid.' This particular one is a precocious little 12-year old Asian girl who just happens to be a computer genius... and the dog is her pet.

Getting back to my statement above about 'repetition being a good thing,' one advantage is that you don't have to construct all your characters from scratch every time you put them into another book. People probably aren't reading your books in a marathon session or in the order you wrote them, so you'll have to do some character establishing, but it's your book, so do the repeating character introductions with any method you feel comfortable with, but please don't fall into the trap of 'B' movies, where one character will say to another, "that's easy for you to say, because you were a special forces marine with explosives training, and all I ever did was translate seven foreign languages for the intelligence department." That's the easy way out, and you'll be much better off defining your characters by their actions than by what other people say about them.

After the first four or five books featuring the same characters, I devised a way to eliminate being forced into thinking up ways to re-introduce the same characters: I started adding an **Introduction** to the book, that started out with "If this is the first Peter Sharp Legal Adventure you're reading, then you might like to know a little about the cast of characters that Peter usually relies upon." I then go on to introduce each character - and the exact same **Introduction** got cut and pasted into every book that followed.

This makes telling your story a lot easier, because you don't have to introduce each character at the first appearance: they're already constructed for you.

Think about a television show like **Law & Order, SVU**. There's a whole group of characters in the squad room at any given time, and during the course of an episode, each one contributes some dialogue. In network television drama, an hour show is only about 44 minutes of actual program, so if you're going to have to spend time establishing the entire cast of characters every week, the shows better be based on *short* stories, because you're never going to fit in all the character establishing and still have enough time for a decent plot with some dialogue in that short period of time.

Chapter Two: Name-Calling

At this point, my team was starting to come into being and it was time to give them names. This can be a problem, because there are a lot of things to avoid when naming a character... and one of them is lawsuits. I wasn't too worried about the kid. Being Asian, I wanted her to have a name that sounded 100% American, but had a hint of Asian ancestry in it, so I finally settled on ***Suzi***. Spelled with the "i" ending, I thought that it would fit in nicely. Having her use only one name also helped out, because there was little chance of a legal conflict with a real person... but I still researched it in advance, as much as I could.

The dog was even easier: being a Saint Bernard, I just called him ***Bernie***, not at all being worried about any lawsuits from dogs who might be reading the books. I explained away the simplicity of his name by mentioning that his real name was only used by the kid: some strange-sounding Chinese word that my lead character didn't understand and couldn't pronounce.

It was a little harder getting a name for my lead character, because he's a professional person, sworn in and licensed to practice law in the State of California, where the stories all take place. This means that if you pick a name of a real California attorney, you're looking for trouble.

One of the real greats, Donald Westlake, had a man named **John Archibald Dortmunder** that he used in 14 novels and 11 short stories. In reality, *Dortmunder* is a pale lager that originated in the industrial city of Dortmund in Germany, but when Westlake saw it advertised on a neon sign, he created the name of his main character... and by that name itself, you should be able to have some idea of the great personality of Donald Westlake, who many authors feel should be immortalized with a statue of his likeness placed in front of every library.

After discovering that my first few dozen names were unusable because of similarity to living attorneys in California and several surrounding states, I got lucky. Using the first and last names of two attorney friends of mine I know (Peter Knecht and Tony Sharp), I created the name ***Peter Sharp***. The only other person of note that I could find with a similar name was a professional athlete in Australia.

Giving names to walk-on characters (guest stars) who will only appear in one book are another problem, especially if they are being painted in a bad light, like being an insane killer. Proper research on Google and Yahoo will help out. A complicated spelling is also a useful tool that leads to a character being referred to only by his or her nickname.

In one of my books the action takes place in a town about 50 miles outside of Los Angeles and the local police chief there is a main character. I drove out there and inquired as to whether or not the police chief or any member of their small force had a name similar to the one I was planning on using for my character, and only finalized its use after they informed me it was safe to use.

The FBI and CIA are quite different. In some of my books Peter runs up against an FBI Special Agent based in their West Los Angeles office. I tried to find out if the name I was using was close to any actual agent there, but they wouldn't give out any information about their agents, so I used the name I had chosen.

The CIA is a special case, and I would advise against using any name for a CIA employee in any book you write. First of all, there's no way you're ever going to get clearance for use of a fictional CIA agent unless you're Tom Clancy or with a major motion picture studio or television network.

Second of all, if you decide to make up a name for a fictional CIA agent, just your luck, it might be close or actually the real name or cover name of an actual CIA agent, and then you're into a Valerie Plame type of situation. Not good. If you have to have someone in the CIA in your story, try not to give that character a name, and simply mention 'the spook,' or some other reference used for a spy.

On second thought, 'spook' might be a bad word to use. If you think differently, you should read the first few chapters of **The Human Stain**.

Now that the characters exist and have names, the next step is to give them some traits, and one thing governing that in my mind was an experience I had many years ago when creating a video on celestial navigation (I guess that by now you know I'm a boating enthusiast). After shooting a program called **Celestial Navigation: Sextant Use & the Sun Noon Shot**, I wanted to market it on the internet, and the best way to do that is getting on the search engines. Everything was going fine until I started getting rejection messages from several search engines, with a form-letter message stating that they "do not accept adult material."

I checked out those search engines and saw that they had plenty of things for children and adults, so I started communicating with them to find out why they rejected my video program. The answer I received from each one of them was that they were 'Christian' search engines, and their filters picked up "s-e-x" in the title word "Sextant," and automatically rejected my submission and sent a message to me.

Everyone knows that the major search engines are Google, Yahoo, Bing and a couple of others... probably fewer than ten, if you're counting. These are the ones that it's vital to be on, so why should I worry about some rinky-dink Christian search engine in Virginia? Simple: I'm a businessman too, and I don't want to start out my fiction writing career by creating something that might offend an important segment of society: readers.

Here are some interesting statistics to keep in mind: in July of 2005, the new Harry Potter book sold 6.9 million copies in its first 24 hours of release. Scholastic Children's Books, the publishers of J.K. Rowling's ***Harry Potter and the Half-Blood Prince***, have increased their print run from 10.8 million to 13.5 million copies. Many of those 13.5 million copies may be going to libraries to be read by many people; many copies will be passed along to friends, and many will be re-sold as used books, which may make the total readership of that one title around 20 million – and no kid can read that book unless he or she knows how to read, so Steve Jobs might have been wrong when he claimed in a pre-iPad/iBook statement that nobody reads anymore.

The point I'm trying to make here is that reading is coming back into fashion, now that new modes of reading (on eReaders, iPhones, on computers) are becoming available, and putting 'adult' material into a book may cut into sales. No parent wants to let a child read a book that has the "F" word in it as many times as Chris Rock or Eddie Murphy uses it in a 60-minute cable television special.

P.S. Many attorney and non-attorney friends told me that they would love having me use their real names my books – even if I made them murderers. Who knew?

Chapter Three: Bringing People to Life

I don't remember Sherlock Holmes, Hercule Poirot, Miss Marple, Nero Wolfe or any of my other fictional heroes ever having a steamy love scene or big shoot-em-up. Their stories were *plot-driven* and they all did quite well in the fiction market, so I thought I'd keep my characters squeaky clean and rely on the quality of the plot to drive the story. As the old saying goes, '*the play's the thing.*'

Yes, I know that Sherlock had a slight abuse problem with cocaine, but in those days it was on the edge of being acceptable. I decided early on that Peter Sharp wouldn't smoke, but did allow him to have an occasional Margarita – or two. A close friend of mine works for the Patrón Spirits Company (makers of tequila) and I had the pleasure of meeting its CEO, John Paul Dejoria, a very pleasant, wealthy man who also owns Paul Mitchell Hair Care Products and numerous other businesses.

While discussing my books with friends, the suggestion was made that as a courtesy to my friends, it could be made with Patrón tequila. This could also be used in the books as a 'way in' for Peter to take a vacation every once in a while and fly over to Hawaii to visit the LaHaina Yacht Club on Maui, where I also happen to be a member... and enjoy their margaritas.

Okay, we now have two main characters, complete with names. One of them drinks a little and the other doesn't. Next I had to construct their relationship and why they are working together, because Peter is not currently married - and when he was, he never had any children... and if he did, because his wife was not Asian, the odds were against a child of that marriage being Chinese like Suzi. I had to create another 'way in' for her character, so I arranged for some events that would allow Peter to 'inherit' her.

Peter had a classmate in law school named Melvin Braunstein who offered to help Peter out after his divorce by giving a job making court appearances. Melvin had been married to a Chinese lady who managed a local Chinese restaurant around the corner from Marina del Rey, California, where the stories are all based.

Because of circumstances that are revealed in the first Peter Sharp Legal Mystery (***Single Jeopardy***), Peter gets appointed as Suzi's legal guardian, so she and the huge dog show up at his boat, suitcase in hand... and once I got them living together, next task in line was to develop their personal relationship.

My problem with the relationship part is that I've never been a parent, and quite honestly have to admit that I haven't got the slightest idea of what a 12-year-old girl might say to a legal guardian that she may not be too fond of... especially one that she knows is not as smart as she is... like most adults she comes in contact with.

The answer was simple: for a large portion of the first book, the kid didn't talk much to Peter. Fortunately, another friend of mine who happens to have five daughters coached me about how those types of creatures interact with adults, so I was able to give the kid some choice lines as the book progressed.

Another major player in the story was required to provide some conflict, and an ex-wife is always a good choice for that part. One of my favorite old Movies was **Adam's Rib**, starring Spencer Tracy as a prosecuting attorney and Katherine Hepburn as his wife, also an attorney. Katherine decides to take up the defense of a woman her husband is prosecuting.

I already had decided to not make Peter Sharp a prosecutor, because defense attorneys are more likeable, unless you're a big fan of the **Law & Order** TV series. If Peter was going to be a defense attorney, then his ex-wife would have to be a prosecutor. This would accomplish several things:

First, it would still leave Peter single and free to flirt with attractive women;

Second, it would provide some personal and courtroom conflict between them; and,

Third, it would be easy to create dialogue between them because although I'm not too sharp in the way little girls talk, I have some expertise in the way that ex-wives do.

These three main characters were introduced early on, so that their relationships could start to mature while the plots thickened and some featured players started to appear. Notice that I used the word "plots" as a plural... more about the need for multiple plots will be discussed later on in this book.

Chapter Four: Resources

There's no way that a crime can be solved without resources... and the most important resource you can have in mystery and detective work is information. Therefore, it's incumbent on any author of crime-solving stories to create some way for the lead characters to get their 'Intel.'

In the **Rockford Files**, Jim Rockford had a friendly police lieutenant. **Columbo** walked around in a trench coat, smoking that smelly cigar and bugging people with 'just one more question.' In **NCIS**, two of the team members are computer experts who 'hack' into places to get their Intel. **Law & Order Criminal Intent** has several brilliant detectives with untapped knowledge about a lot of subjects, and a keen talent for observation... and they also use computers quite well.

The bottom line is that every crime-solver needs some way to get the facts to use in making deductions about who the guilty person. Most of the time, a lot depends on finding Motive, and that's why quite often at the end of a story you'll learn that the person who seemed to have absolutely no motive at all was really the guilty party.

In my Legal Mystery Series, Peter Sharp is not an ex-cop (that plot device has been overdone), so he doesn't have any connections with the police department. His ex-wife is a prosecutor, and most of the time she's looking for some way to pin something on her good-for-nothing defense attorney ex-husband, so there's no help there. The kid is only twelve and rarely leaves the boat, so that looks like another dead end for intelligence gathering.

Nero Wolfe had his outside leg-man Archie Goodwin; *Sherlock Holmes* had his band of street urchins, the Baker Street Irregulars; big-shot movie and television defense attorneys have unlimited budgets and private investigators out there tailing people and going through garbage. I had to figure out some way for Peter Sharp to get some Intel on the cases he works on, but only a small group of trusted beings to choose from: the kid and the dog.

Given my scant number of selections, I decided to go with the kid. She's already been established as a computer genius, so I embellished her abilities by strengthening her relationship with Peter's ex-wife Myra, the prosecutor. This would give her someone to talk to other than Peter, with whom her relationship was slightly strained due to their forced legal/living situation created by the court.

Another benefit to having Suzi and Myra get chummy was to create a secret agenda for the kid: she constantly tries to figure out some way to get Peter and Myra back together again, so that she'll have a full family to live with... and while an occasionally house-guest of Myra's, Suzi can have an opportunity to 'look' at some crime-fighting software on Myra's computer – programs not available to the general public.

Much like the old TV show **Remington Steele**, I established Suzi as the probable brains behind Peter's little law firm, but still needed a couple of fill-in characters to build side-plots on, and three of them came into being during the first book.

Stuart Schwartzman: an old friend of Peter's who starts out a little down on his luck, but because of Peter's clever maneuvering to settle legal matters for him, and his own entrepreneurial talent, Stuart provides some nice cut-away material, and his frequent attempts to start new businesses provide some good material on its own.

Jack Bibberman: a clerk at a private post-office place who provides some extremely helpful information to Peter on one case. To show his appreciation, Peter turns Jack into the firm's private snoop, sending him out to sneak around to gather Intel.

Miguel Herrera: This may sound a little macabre, but Miguel owns a company called 800Autopsy (that's also his phone number). Miguel is a former coroner's assistant who decided to go out on his own, and now operates a private autopsy business, serving insurance companies and medical malpractice lawyers. His employees are all former CSI people who provide technical assistance to Peter and Suzi on their cases.

[Side note: Miguel isn't his real name, but this character is an actual person, based on a real California business with the same name and telephone number as the one used in the book – with his permission]

Miguel brings another dimension to the story, because his firm can provide Peter and Suzi with the same type of services that the people on the **CSI** shows do: DNA, fingerprint, ballistics, etc.

With the resources all in place, it's now time to start getting in some cases that need solving, and if this process sounds like the construction of a building, it's supposed to. These characters are going to be brought back in story after story, and if the foundation is weak, the building won't last through the entire series.

Chapter Five: The Clients

L egal cases for a fictional detective story are a lot like peanuts or potato chips: you can't eat just one.

If you watch a one-hour episodic television show about cops and robbers, you will usually see at least two plot lines develop. They don't have to be 'major' plot lines: one will no doubt chronicle catching the main bad guy (usually the episode's 'guest star'), and the other one will be a minor plot point that will focus on one of several other issues and/or conflicts:

An outside relationship of one of the cast members;

A relationship between two cast members;

A conflict between a cast member and a superior officer;

A minor case involving one cast member trying to unofficially help a friend;

An internal affairs investigation about alleged inappropriate behavior of a cast member while on duty;

Behavior of a guest star with accomplices;

Competition between police agencies (local police –vs- federal officers);

Physical illness, stress, addiction, or borderline legal behavior of a featured cast member.

These are just a few of the side plots that can pop up in a long-form (one-hour program) television police/ law/crime drama. It's a lot like the old cowboy movies where there were only a limited number of plots to choose from: rustlers, cowboys/sheepherders, the gold claim, water rights, a 'town tamer,' the fastest gun, the saloon gambler, a roving gang of bank, stage, or train robbers, a bounty hunter, railroad rights of way, North/South, the posse search, lynch mobs, or cowboys/Indians. Did I leave any out?

***

A well constructed long form drama and especially a novel should have a minimum of two or three plot lines, lest it be considered too 'linear.' In order for several plot lines to exist, clients or friends must often be brought into the story. That's why I tried to populate my Legal Mystery series with a small but tight group of distinct personalities right at the beginning. They are the building blocks of the story, and can also be good sources of bringing cases in.

In my books, Peter and Suzi (and the dog) live on a yacht in Marina del Rey, California, and several times Peter takes on a case at the urging of Suzi trying to help a friend's parent or a dock neighbor.

Peter's friend Stuart is always starting new businesses that occasionally run into legal problems.

I also brought in an insurance company that Peter occasionally does some defense work for, and in a couple of instances, Peter's ex-wife Myra arranged for him to receive paid court appointments to defend people on criminal cases that she felt were 'winners,' and would give her a chance to demolish her ex-husband in court.

There is also a rare occasion in three of the books when Peter's ex-wife asks a favor – and in one book they even wind up working together on a case.

Another matter that can be a side-plot is Suzi's schooling. She is home-schooled, but we never see a teacher. Her grades on the tests that the Board of Education had her take were so high, that they require her to come downtown once a quarter to take the tests in a proctored situation. This frequent event gives the characters a chance to drive downtown together, and Suzi always convinces Myra to join them after the test so that they can all have lunch together.

See what I mean? Lots of choices, lots of ways to get clients in, and plenty of opportunity to get away from the main plot to redirect focus to a side plot... a 'thread' that weaves its way through the book, popping up here and there to provide a brief 'breakaway' from the main plot, until it is finally resolved.

Chapter Six: ...by Any Other Name

Now that you can see what it takes to put a cast together and give them some resource methods, you should be thinking about what your story will be about... and that's a good time to start thinking about a working title.

Here are the fifteen titles in my *Peter Sharp Legal Mystery Series*:

Single Jeopardy
...by Reason of Sanity
A Class Action
Conspiracy of Innocence
...Until Proven Innocent
The Common Law
The Magician's Legacy
The Reluctant Jurist
The Final Case
An Element of Peril
A Good Alibi
Legally Dead
How to Rob a Bank
Murder Under Way
The Sherlock Holmes Caper

Note the legal and/or crime theme present in most of the titles. If you do a series of books, by the time you've polished off six in the series, people will know what type of book to expect even if some element of the law isn't in the main title.

However, just to play safe, the title of each one of my books has a sub-title that's included in all of the eBook listings. For example, the fourth book in the series has a full title of **Conspiracy of Innocence: Peter Sharp Legal Mystery #4.** There's no escaping the fact that it's a Peter Sharp book, and it now also gets more exposure for the series in the search engines.

And now, here's a little secret tip that I've been following right from the first book: quite often I create the title first, before the book is written. Yeah, I know, it sounds crazy – but if you can figure out how to make up a good title for a mystery/crime/detective novel that hasn't been used by anyone else in the past 50 years, use it! Don't worry about relevance to your story, because if you can't figure out a way to work a word like "Crime," "Murder," or "Gun" into your mystery, then instead of writing you should consider plumbing for a career. One well-known author, the late Frank McCourt, used the last word of one of his books as the title.

Every one of my titles could be used on any one of the other books by the simple device of having a client ask a question about some point of law, and then by working the title into the answer. It can also be worked into a conversation here and there, so that it starts to become relevant to the story – even if only by reference. For example, every crime novel could have the words "a good alibi" in it somewhere.

29

And here's another 'inside' secret I found out from my publisher, Magic Lamp Press: one of their authors (Nick Shoveen) wrote a book about low-budget film production. They couldn't give the darn thing away. It dangled in the wind on Amazon in both print and eBook versions for six months without one sale.

The author got a bright idea: he added a few pages and created a chapter on the specific things to watch out for when producing an 'adult' film. Things like making sure the girls are not under age, verifying authenticity of driver's license and social security numbers and getting releases signed properly.

At the end of the book he inserted a small section about local and federal laws with respect to pornography, and then changed the title of the book to ***How to be a Porno Producer***. That title is now his second-best selling title in both print and eBook versions.

I'm sure you noticed that I said his Porno Producer title is now his second-best selling title, so I have a feeling you'd like to hear about his #1 best-seller. Okay, here it is.

Taking the unemployment rate into consideration, he wrote a book on how to set up a small business that can be run out of a person's residence. Home businesses are very popular now, so he did some research and included in the book things like how to protect yourself from people knowing you're working out of your second bedroom: getting a P.O. box at a place like the UPS store, where a street address can be used in your address; getting an economical incoming toll-free 800 line that runs into your existing phone line, plus many other helpful suggestions on accounting, taxes, etc.

Under its original title, this book was as successful as the porno producer book was before the title was changed. Nada. Zip. Nothing. No sales at all.

Remembering how changing the name of the other book worked out for him, he decided to add a chapter or two about another type of home-based business and changed the title of the book. It is now his #1 best-seller under the title of **The Phone Sex Manual**.

The publisher reasoned that one of the reasons these books are so popular is not only because of the hint of sexual content, but because they are great novelty gift books... the type of thing you give to a person who has everything. And in addition to that, there isn't one 'dirty' word in either of these books: they are strictly serious how-to business books, so that parents don't have to worry about one of their kids picking one up and reading it. I'm pretty sure that neither one of these titles will ever make it onto the Christian search engines, but they'll still turn in some attractive sales numbers.

Chapter Seven: Working Backwards

When Arthur Conan Doyle started his medical practice, he didn't do very well. In fact, it's reported that he had so few patients, that in order to fill his spare time, he started writing a story about a detective named Sherlock Holmes.

Similarly, when I first started my law practice, I too had a lot of time on my hands, so I spent several hours a day doing crossword puzzles. The **Los Angeles Times** had one every day that I was able to finish most of the time, and a paper in the San Fernando Valley published the **New York Times**' daily puzzle - that I finished once or twice a year [Wil Shortz is an evil person].

After a while, I became pretty good at solving them and thought 'Gee, I'll bet I could create one of these." Well, to make a long story short (something a novelist should never say), after a month or so practicing construction, I started to sell my puzzles to local publications, each one containing a few words that fit into the publication's theme.

For a while, I contributed my crossword creations to the monthly California State Bar publication that every lawyer in the state received free as part of their Bar membership.

Many of my friends knew that I was making and selling these puzzles, and the most frequently asked question I fielded was "how the heck do you do that?"

The answer was simple, and was always the same: "I work backwards. First, I take a blank puzzle and start to fill in the blanks so that words are formed up and down. When that's done, I put numbers in where they should go and then start to think up clever and often misleading clues."

I didn't know it at the time, but that's the same principle I was to use several times in my career. Another time I talked about it was when I was teaching a class in legal writing to a class of law students.

Back when I took the California Bar exam, they used to contain some essay questions, and the assigned grader for each question probably had a couple of thousand answers to read, all submitted by desperate law students hoping to pass the bar and become lawyers.

Here's the advice I gave them, based on the time allotted in those days: You're going to have about 3-½ hours to answer four questions, and that breaks down to about 52-½ minutes for each question – so here's what you do. Make sure you bring a little timer with you, and leave about an inch or so blank at the top of your answer.

Then, for the next 45 minutes, go ahead with your incoherent babbling about the question, and try to hit all the issues you think are involved.

33

By the time you've spent 45 minutes trying to answer the question, you should have a pretty good idea of the proper order that those things should have been brought up in your answer, but it's way too late to change things now, so – go back to that blank inch at the top of your answer and fill it in with the issues in the proper way that you feel they should have been discussed, but make sure to mention that "in order to answer this question properly, the following issues should be covered in this sequence."

If you state the issues properly and in the proper order, and briefly mention pertinent law and suggested legal conclusions, the reader will see that right off the bat, before even starting to read your answer, that you have a good comprehension of what the answer should be, the order the issues should be addressed, and the legal conclusions.

Taking into consideration that the graders were beginning lawyers themselves and only getting paid less than a buck to grade each question, once they see how you seemed to have organized your complete answer in advance, and apparently spotted each important issue right off the bat, the odds are that they'll toss your paper onto the 'pass' file. It worked for me, and it worked for my students. We all went on to practice law.

The next time that principle came up was when I started to write mystery stories. It's just like being a magician. First, you go to the magic shop and buy a great trick. Then you practice doing it until it becomes second nature. Last, you create the opening patter you'll be using when introducing the trick to your audience. You work backwards, whether it's answering a bar question, creating a crossword puzzle, a magic trick, or a mystery novel.

Of course I don't mean that you write the book backwards, because you'd have to be fluent in Hebrew to do it that way (in that language they write from right to left). I mean you should know how the bad guy did the crime, how he escaped and what clues he unwittingly left behind, before you write yourself into a corner by not being able to figure out how to solve the crime.

Here's an example I've seen numerous times during the past twenty years. In one movie, a guy died in a locked room, so when they had to break the door down to get into the crime scene, they saw him lying on the floor. A doctor told everyone to stand back while he rushed to the man, bent down next to him and then slowly stood up, letting everyone there know that they were too late... the man was already dead – thereby creating the big mystery of how he could have been murdered in that completely locked room.

The trick? It's simple. The doctor was the killer. He drugged the victim's coffee so that he would remain conscious for a while after he locked everyone out of his private study, and also talk to someone on the phone, establishing that he was still alive after locking everyone out.

Soon the drugs took effect and the victim passed out, but was still alive. The killer didn't want him to die of poison, because that might have led the investigation to the doctor. Instead, after they broke into the room, the doctor rushed over the victim, and after telling everyone to 'stand back,' he bent down, and while appearing to examine the victim, he was actually smothering him to death.

The last time I saw a similar plot stunt like that was on an episode of **Monk**, just last year. It's a good one, and been done many times before... but if you're going to use that plot device, you have to work backwards. First you have to figure out how to kill the victim quickly, without anyone noticing. Then, you have to create the situation that leaves the victim in the secluded or locked room, still communicating with people on the outside, to establish life after the locks are activated.

Once you've got those two elements covered, you can start to create your story and make sure that the killer has absolutely no *apparent* motive... but there either has to be a mistake the criminal made, or a clue that only your crime-solver will notice that gives some believable way to solve the crime.

What I've been describing above are variations on what's known in the business as a 'locked-room' mystery, my favorite kind, and one that I created in my book #7, **The Magician's Legacy** that surprises absolutely everyone who reads it. I did another version in #14, **Murder Under Way**, when a man is killed in his boat at sea... even though he's alone in the boat.

Sometimes it becomes difficult to weave the plot elements so that they fit together nicely. In one of my books I had one heck of a time trying to figure out how to kill a guy, so I did what I always try to do when I'm up against a brick plot wall like that – I go for a long walk, from my boat out to the beach, and then on a course that covers about three miles.

There have been times when I was so deep in thought, that when I returned to my boat I wondered if I actually did the entire walk, and only confirmed it by looking at my wristwatch set to the stopwatch function.

One time during my walk I received a cell phone call from another writer I know, and spent the better part of about twenty minutes trying to explain the trouble I was having trying to kill this guy. I was so involved in the conversation that I didn't realize how my voice must have been carrying to the people I was walking near on the beach's boardwalk. I think that if that telephone conversation would have been heard any place other than where I was, on the Venice Beach Boardwalk, I probably would have had some uniformed police stopping me for an explanation about the planned murder.

Keep in mind my tip about walking: it works wonders when you've got a crime to plan… and if you're going to be talking to yourself, try to not do it out loud.

Chapter Eight: Know Your Limitations

One of my favorite movie lines was spoken by the famous philosopher D.H. (Dirty Harry) Calahan in the last scene of the motion picture ***Magnum Force***, as Clint Eastwood watches Hal Holbrook, the crooked police chief, drive away after threatening to frame Dirty Harry for murdering police officers.

What Holbrook didn't know was that there was a time bomb in the vehicle he took away from Eastwood, and when Dirty Harry exited the car, he armed the bomb.

A minute or so later, as the crooked police chief drove off into the distance, we see the car explode, obviously killing the bad cop. Eastwood's Dirty Harry character, with that familiar grimace on his face, utters, "Man's got to know his limitations."

The same applies to you as a mystery writer. If you don't know anything about poisons, don't try to be another Agatha Christie. If you've never been to Europe, don't put your characters there. If you don't know anything about the law, don't write a legal mystery (I don't need the competition).

Everyone thinks the grass is greener on the other side, but you can usually find enough to write about in your own back yard. Write about something you know about.

A friend of mine is a dentist, so he created a story about a company that put nano-tracking material into the stuff they fill cavities with. You don't have to rattle off a bunch of stuff that nobody will understand, just to show how smart you are: a simple explanation of some things will be greatly appreciated by the reading public.

People want to learn. They are fascinated with new, interesting information. Take a look at the success of the **CSI** franchise on CBS. It's gotten to a point where juries hearing actual cases in courtrooms nowadays seem to be disappointed with the prosecution fails to call a CSI expert in to show how they tracked the defendant by some small trace evidence they found. The public actually believes that the computer will say "Positive Match" on the screen when an identical fingerprint is found, when in actuality, all the computer can do is make a match on similar 'points' with respect to loops, whirls, hooks, and other distinguishing characteristics of a fingerprint. [Each jurisdiction has a threshold number of 'matching qualities' before they will deem it statistically significant enough to consider the prints a 'most probable positive match']

If you're writing about something you know, try to make it interesting by inserting bits of information, simply explained, wherever it might be relevant. When the reader finishes your book, having enjoyed the plot and

39

also *learned* something will add to their enjoyment and encourage them to read another one of your books.

In my books, I established Peter's friend Stuart as a correspondence school law student who is constantly questioning Peter about some aspect of the law in whatever case he's working on... and Peter usually obliges, with a simple explanation of the legal principles involve. Stuart appreciates it, and so do the readers.

If you're going to stray from your own comfort zone, make it concern things you are familiar with. In my stories, Peter Sharp lives on a yacht, but it stays in its slip, because he gets seasick easily. Also, he hasn't the slightest idea of even how to start the engines, and certainly would never be able to steer the thing if it got started.

In real life, I've been boating for several decades and have taught numerous boat owners how to drive their newly-acquired yachts, up to 84 feet (the largest one I ever skippered). I drive a small car, because I can't stand those huge things that soccer moms feel they need to drop their small child off for a ballet lesson... but Peter Sharp loves his big yellow Hummer. Not an H2 or wussy H3, but one of the huge original Hummers – the first 8-foot wide model that was de-militarized and painted shiny for domestic consumption.

I sent a copy of my first book to a writer friend of mine. He read it (and I read his) and then we met for lunch to trade notes. When we left the restaurant together, he saw that I had found a parking space right in front of the restaurant and when he saw me open my car door he asked "You're driving that little thing? Where's your Hummer, back at the boat?"

I was flattered. He obviously thought that the Hummer-driving part of my book was partly autobiographical, and he was quite surprised when I told him that it was Peter Sharp who drove the Hummer, not me... and that I wouldn't have one of those huge gas-guzzling trucks if they gave it to me.

No matter what subject you're going to use as a backdrop for your book, you can't be expected to know everything about everything, so be prepared to do some research. If you have access to the internet, you can learn a lot about anything you're writing about by using Google, Wikipedia, journals, etc.

In one of my books, a client had amnesia, so I re-searched the most common forms of the ailment, so I could write about the client's doctor explaining amnesia to Peter. Researched material appears in every book I write, and I spend a great deal of time trying to 'dumb it down' so that the reader's eyes don't start to glaze over when the explanation starts.

No matter what your life background is, you must also have a basic knowledge of how to get it from your head onto the page, and the one thing you should read first (even before my books) is what has been referred to for many years as 'the little book' but it's real title is **The Elements of Style**. You can order it from Amazon, where new and used versions are being sold for as little as $1.00

And, if you'd like to read the best book in the world when it comes to punctuation use, I strongly suggest Lynne Truss' definitive and humorous book, **Eats Shoots & Leaves**. It's also available inexpensively at Amazon.

You may not think that this has much to do with the writing of a mystery, but if you don't have a command of the English language (and proper punctuation is a must) you'll be a huge disappointment to any discriminating reader – therefore, I have decided to show you two sample paragraphs from Lynne Truss' book. They are both the same words, but have been punctuated differently – thereby giving them completely different meanings.

Here's the first paragraph: a very romantic note from Jill to Jack:

Dear Jack,
I want a man who knows what love is all about. You are generous, kind, thoughtful. People who are not like you admit to being useless and inferior. You have ruined me for other men. I yearn for you. I have no feelings whatsoever when we're apart. I can be forever happy – will you let me be yours?   Jill

Now here's the second paragraph: exact same words, but punctuated differently: you may note a slightly different meaning:

Dear Jack,
I want a man who knows what love is. All about you are generous, kind, thoughtful people, who are not like you. Admit to being useless and inferior. You have ruined me. For other men I yearn! For you I have no feelings whatsoever. When we're apart I can be forever happy. Will you let me be? Yours, Jill

Chapter Nine: Finding Your Voice

Who's telling the story in your book? Is it one of the characters in the book? Is it you? Is it a third-party narrator? And what is the tense used? Is it a story about things that happened, or is it a real-time narrative about things that are happening as the story-teller is experiencing them?

Each one of those choices will require a different technique, different ways of presenting dialogue, and different ways of finding facts.

In my books, the stories are all present-tense, first person. The speaker is Peter Sharp and he is giving a minute-by-minute account of things as they happen. I chose this method mainly because I'm lazy. If you use my method, doing a conversation between your narrator and another person is a lot easier because you don't have to worry too much about the reader getting confused about exactly who is talking at any given time.

If Peter is talking to Stuart, every once in a while he'll say something like "I don't know, Stu..." and that's a clear signal Peter is speaking, and not Stuart.

Of course whatever method you choose will also have its downside. If you're using a first person present tense method like mine, you are restricted to telling only what your narrator can see. If you want to bring in things that happened outside the narrator's point of view, it must be presented as someone telling it to your narrator, or your main voice person seeing it on television reading it in the newspaper or going online and seeing it.

Another reason I like it is because it gives me an opportunity to let the reader know what's going on in Peter's mind. His thoughts are fully explored. In several of the books, when Peter thinks he's got the entire case all figured out (he's usually wrong), he'll call Bernie the dog in and present the case to him... and for the low price of one dog biscuit, the dog will sit there and listen to the entire presentation without disagreeing once.

Another thing I like about first-person present-tense narration is that for me, it's easier to build suspense.

Take these two examples for instance:
"A well-dressed man walks into the bar. The bartender doesn't know that the man is wearing a shoulder holster."

Or,

"I'm standing next to the cigarette machine near the door and notice that a well-dressed man is entering the bar. He stops for a moment to light his cigarette and I can't help but notice that he's wearing a shoulder holster than contains what looks like a very large revolver. I want to signal the bartender that there's an armed man approaching the bar, but can't attract his attention... I suddenly think of a way we can make eye contact, so that I can use my *Charades* skill to let him know..."

See what I mean? If you're in the middle of what's going on, you can help build the tension with your own thoughts and fears... and here's a tip you might consider, and why I prefer the present-tense first-person style: I've always had the long-range plan of having my books presented in three different formats: print, ebooks, and as audiobooks – and the first-person style is a lot more economical to do, and if you've got the stamina to do it, you can also advertise it as "being read by the author."

Another tip is that one of the best devices for building tension is a 'ticking clock,' and I'll go into that in more detail later in Chapter Eleven.

Chapter Ten: Variety - the Spice of Life

Once you've settled on a voice and a tense, here's something to avoid about 'voices:' don't make them all the same – like yours.

If you're using a program like Microsoft Word, you'll be in a constant battle with the spell-check and grammar functions when trying to do dialects, but it's worth it. For goodness sake, please remember to make your cast of characters each a little different.

In my books, Peter is an attorney, so he has to sound like an educated person, but his fault is missing the point quite often.

His ex-wife Myra is also educated, but she's a hard-driven prosecutor with absolutely no sense of humor, and can be quite sarcastic at times, especially itwhen speaking to her ex-husband Peter.

The kid is obviously the smartest of them all, and she doesn't waste time with people she feels are a great deal beneath her when it comes to intelligence and logic. She has a tendency to 'talk down' even to the adults when they just 'don't get it' about something that she recognizes intuitively. It's not uncommon for her to simply do a young girls' 'eye-roll' in frustration and then just turn around and walk out of the room, followed by the beast Bernie.

Having each cast member speak a little differently also makes conversations between more than two people a lot easier for the reader to follow.

There's an old theater device called the 'feather duster.' Here's a typical example of it: the curtain goes up on Act I and we see a maid using a feather duster in what looks like the entryway of a beautiful mansion. The telephone rings and is answered by the maid, who says, "No, the senator isn't in; he's at the opera with his wife. They're honoring him there this evening because his donation built the new stage they're performing on." She hangs up, but while using that feather duster she managed to set up the main character of the play by telling you about him during the phone call.

You can use methods like that by incorporating information into the dialogue between people, but I think that letting the characters' actions describe them much better than someone's dialogue about them... and that's a lot easier to do in writing than on the stage, because it's hard to 'act' out some complicated thought that's on one's mind.

Another thing to watch out for is going over the top with character idiosyncrasies, in a desperate effort to make a character's persona unique. Just a little will be fine. Readers appreciate subtle nuances. It gives them the feeling that they're the only ones who picked up on it, even more so than other people reading the exact same words.

The same principles apply when giving physical descriptions about people or places. A book is really a graphic presentation, because as each reader goes through your words, they're mentally seeing a motion picture of what they're reading. Just give them a hint of the character and let them build the rest by themselves, in their own minds.

Chapter Eleven: Tension

Keeping the readers in tension is the best way to turn your book into a 'page-turner.' Another device I use in print versions is the 'next even page' break while formatting. This means that if a chapter ends on an even page, usually on the left side of the open book, the next chapter will not start on the next page visible on the right side of the book. Instead, the reader will be forced to turn the page to see the next chapter start on the top of the left side of the book.

Think of it this way: you don't want to spoil the reader's experience. Here's an example: at the end of a chapter, you try to insert a bit of a 'cliff-hanger' by having your hero dropped down into a well. While down there, he realizes that it will be impossible for him to escape without some outside help – and because there is nobody around, there's a good chance that he will perish.

This chapter ends on an even page. The reader is worried about the hero, and glances over to the odd page on the right side of the open book, and sees that the next chapter starts with the words "Once out of the well…"

See what I mean? It would have been a better reading experience if the reader had to turn that page over to see the beginning of the next chapter. That's what makes the book a 'page-turner.'

I've already mentioned the ticking clock method, and the most direct example of it is like the end of a typical James Bond movie, when he must disarm the big bomb that its timerindicates is set to go off in less than a minute.

Another popular ticking clock device is the search for a kidnap victim that is in danger dying for lack of medicine, buried underground or in some other sort of peril that will be fatal if not discovered.

Personally, I prefer a more subtle approach to the ticking clock – an approaching trial date, with suspense building because each day as that trial becomes more imminent, Peter realizes how embarrassed he'll be in court because he hasn't yet figured out a decent defense.

In a **non**-Peter Sharp screenplay I wrote some time ago, the clock was running because a guy had to get married by a certain date in order to collect an inheritance... and adding suspense to the story was the fact that they were unaware that the provision of the deceased's will containing that requirement was written while the wealthy old man was on vacation, and unbeknownst to the characters, the controlling time was in the time zone of the decedent's, and not in the time zone that the heirs were in.

The readers knew that the real deadline was an hour before everyone else thought it was, but the characters in the book didn't know it. This kept the book's cast cool and collected, and forced the reader to shout at the book "hurry up, or it'll be too late!"

Sexual tension can also be interesting and captivate the readers... and it doesn't have to be between lovers. In my books, there's constant sexual tension between Peter and his ex-wife. If I've done it correctly, the readers are always wondering if the two of them are going to get back together again. He's for it, but I think she protests a little too much, which either means that she's really not interested, or that there's actually a chance for the two of them some time down the road.

The tension between them crops up at times when Myra finds out that Peter is dating another woman, and can't seem to stop herself from making comments about the non-competition, like "she's not that good of a city attorney." The comments aren't vicious, but they're slightly on the unfavorable side... enough to give a slight hint of jealousy, but not enough to hang your hat on.

Non-sexual tension can also be effective when it's between adversaries. It rears its ugly head when Peter and Myra face off against each other in court, and also can be seen between Peter and whatever devious or incompetent adversary he's up against.

Remember – there should be some conflict in your book and depending on whether you want a feel-good book or not, the bad guy might get what's coming to him at the end.

A television program that appears every week for a whole season of up to 20 episodes doesn't have to resolve every conflict by the end of each episode. Some shows will stagger the conflict conclusions so that one from last week concludes this week, while a new one starts that might not conclude for several episodes.

The ones that drag out are usually when the protagonists are after a serial killer from week-to-week, or when some internal affairs investigation unit is pestering them and interviewing a different cast member each week.

That might work it television, but it doesn't play very well in a book. Sometimes a reader will feel slighted if you don't close up all the loose ends by the last page. They may not mind being expected to watch another TV episode next week, because it's free, and if they like the show they're probably planning to watch it on a regular basis anyway. It won't work that well in a book. Try to give the reader some closure by the end of your story.

You don't necessarily have to have the good guy gloating over the bad guy's downfall. The reader will enjoy the closure with or without the gloating. They'll know that good triumphs over evil – even if it's not in a crime setting. It can be any situation with a not-so-nice person tormenting a nice person.

Chapter Twelve: The Butler Did It

Yeah, I know – that's a corny chapter heading, but it's the title I've always wanted to use for a book about a murder in a house where there's also a butler on duty. Last time I checked Amazon.com there were about two dozen books (including some plays) with that title, but I'm still not discouraged.

The real point I'd like to make in this chapter is that if you're writing a mystery, you have to decide what type it will be. They fall into several popular categories:

Whodunnit type: - The detective must figure out who the guilty person is;

Columbo type: - We know right from the beginning who done it – it's the detective's job to figure out how to prove it and to get the perp to confess.
[Please note that this is very similar to the methods police detective Petrovich used in Dostoevsky's **Crime and Punishment,** to finally get student Raskolnikov to confess to killing a pawnbroker].

How'd he do it? Type : - The impossible crime. It may look like an accident or suicide, but the hero thinks it was murder.

<u>Locked-Room type</u>: - How did whoever did it get in and out of the room?

<u>Good Alibi type</u> : - We think we know who did it, but he's got an iron-clad alibi

<u>Secret Motive type</u>: - Who would have wanted to do this crime? Look for the person with no apparent motive.

At one time or another I've used all of the above – and then some.

Sometimes you can have a mystery that's disguised as a non-mystery. A great TV example of this is the popular medical show ***House***, starring Hugh Laurie. Most people think that any mystery in the show is about the strange illness affecting the patient of the week, until Dr. Gregory House figures out that all that is required is an aspirin or two. He's always right, and the deathly ill patient usually walks out of the hospital at the end of the episode... but that's not the mystery portion of the show.

If you take a really close look at the show, you may notice that House is really a take-off on Sherlock Holmes. It's House instead of Holmes. The sidekick is Wilson, instead of Watson. He doesn't play violin, but he does play guitar and piano. He doesn't abuse cocaine, but he does abuse Vicodin.

In first two seasons, House lived in apartment 221 (as in Holmes' 221-B Baker Street). Sherlock Holmes could look at a stranger and tell you all about him: House does the same thing when he works in the hospital's clinic, diagnosing the patients by observing them… and they show amazement at his correct assumptions about them the same way that Dr. Watson used to be amazed at Holmes' powers of observation.

And there's really no need for violence to be shown. I've been watching ***Law & Order Criminal Intent*** for many seasons now, and like ***Monk***, it's one of the most intellectual detective series I've seen.

No matter what type of mystery story you're telling the one rule I like to see strictly adhered to is 'no secrets.' The reader should be privy to all the clues that the hero is privy to. There should never be some information that comes up in the end of the story that the hero learns because of a telegraph he sent earlier in the story that we weren't told about. That's the one thing that bothered me about the Sherlock Holmes stories. Too often he would get some Intel from a source that we didn't know about, and he used that info to solve the crime. The only time we find out about this previously undisclosed source of information is at the end, when he explains the solution to Dr. Watson. Not fair. That's cheating.

In the mystery stories I've written, we all see the clues, and in my promotional material I urge prospective readers to see if they can solve the crime before Suzi, a twelve-year-old girl can. I'll bet parents have given copies of my book to their precocious daughters to read.

Of course nobody is really matching wits with a little girl: they're really competing with an experienced mystery writer who has spent a great deal of time working backwards to make a crime match up to a pre-ordained solution, and every word spoken by the young girl is put in her mouth by an adult writer... but that's our secret – from one writer to another.

Chapter Thirteen:
Putting it on Paper (or on E-ink)

Okay. It's time to stop talking about how to do it and show you how it's supposed to be done, along with a commentary about why certain plot decisions were made.

Fortunately, we have fourteen ready-made examples to work with, and the convenience of having the author present (me) to justify each plot decision.

At this point I'd like to stress how digital printing has revolutionized the publishing industry. Here's one big example: we started printing our books digitally with CreateSpace, a POD (**P**rint **O**n **D**emand) division of Amazon.com. Doing it this way allowed us to print as few as 1 book at a time, and Amazon took all of our orders and did the shipping, then paying us a royalty on each book sold.

Each of the back covers we designed for the books had, in addition to a blurb about the book, a list of all the books in our series – but when the first book came out, there was no series – that was the only book. (***Single Jeopardy*** – Peter Sharp Legal Mystery #1)

As each new book in the series was introduced, by taking advantage of the new digital printing technology, we were able to go back into our files and update each preceding back cover and each interior listing page to add the newly published title – and then submit the revised files for our print and eBook listings.

I mention this to you because when you finish your first book, it's nice to have a print copy to show around, so my suggestion to you is: get it onto CreateSpace as a print version and at the same time get it into their Kindle listings as an eBook. Order just one print proof – there's no time limit. You can keep the unapproved proof as long as you want and use it for proof-reading, editing, etc. When you've finally got the manuscript in the shape you want it to be in, submit a new interior text file for the print version and another one for the eBook.

You can make instant changes to the eBook, but changes to the print version will require taking the book off of the 'active' list while changes are made in Amazon's file, a proof is ordered and received (takes about 10 days) and the proof is approved, to have it become active for sale once again.

If I remember correctly, CreateSpace charges about 1.3¢ per page, plus 90¢, so a 200-page book will cost about $3.50 for the printing and another $3.61 to have them mail it to you, so getting one book will cost you a little over seven dollars. But, once your book is approved and you'd like to order more of them for friends, local bookstores, agents, etc, the shipping costs for 20 books is only about 2 or 3 dollars more.

And here's another tip: they will give you a choice of shipping methods: take the cheapest one. We experimented with each of the methods, and the least expensive was printed, shipped to us and arrived at our office exactly 1 business week after ordering it, so it's just not worth the money to pay extra for expedited delivery.

Below is a copy of their shipping selection info. This was taken off of their page on Sunday, January 24, 2010 – so you can see what their estimated delivery dates are.

Please select a shipping speed:

⊙   Economy Shipping **$3.61** Estimated Arrival Date: **Mon, Feb 15, 2010**

○   Standard Shipping **$6.39** Estimated Arrival Date: **Tue, Feb 09, 2010**

○   Express Shipping **$25.23** Estimated Arrival Date: **Tue, Feb 02, 2010**

○   Priority Shipping **$28.46** Estimated Arrival Date: **Mon, Feb 01, 2010**

If their past performance means anything (tried it about 5 time over a couple of months), a book ordered on Monday, January 25th will arrive at our offices on Monday, February 1st – the   exact same day they promise you'll get it if you pay $28.46 for their Priority Shipping.

If J.K. Rowling decides to self-publish her ***Harry Potter*** series with CreateSpace as paperbacks, the printing of 5 or 10 million copies might slow down their production schedule a little... but I wouldn't worry about that for a while.

Bottom line: pick the cheapest way. It'll probably get there just as fast and you'll save money.

Chapter Fourteen: The First Book

I started out my mystery series with a book that acts like the 'pilot' for a television series. In TV, the pilot is usually a little longer than the regular programs because they like to have an extra hour to develop the lead characters that will be continuing in each of the episodes.

I did the same for my fist book, and it wound up being almost 85,000 words, but that's okay because each continuing character also had a 'back' story that needed telling.

[*Shameless plug: all 15 of the books in my series can be seen at* **www.LegalMystery.com**]

We'll be discussing various plot devices in the series, but there will be no need for a 'spoiler alert,' because nothing will be given away. That's not what an author is supposed to do: if someone wants to know how your hero got out of the well, politely tell them "gee, it's been so long since I wrote that, I just don't remember how he did it, but I know for sure that it's in the book."

****

<u>Not all Trivia is bad</u>. Remember the successful ½-hour television show ***Cheers***? (It's still running on cable, so I guess it's not too ancient a reference to make). One of the cast members was named Cliff Clavin, and the thing he was always doing (that some bar patrons found annoying) was bringing up trivia that had little or nothing to do with whatever was relevant at the time. That device was used successfully to strengthen the persona of that cast member, and as a way to let fellow cast members react to his trivia with clever lines and insults.

Cliff's trivia was designed to be irrelevant and annoying and it served its purpose as a comedic device... but if you're writing a novel, ***relevant*** trivia can be a good thing. Here's an example of some trivia I inserted into one of the books (I forget which one): someone asks Peter Sharp to remind him of the name of the Chief Justice of the U.S. Supreme Court, and Peter's answer is "we don't have one."

Most people would think (presently) that the correct answer to that question is Chief Justice John Roberts – but that's a wrong answer. Peter's answer that 'we don't have one' is the correct answer. Why? Because there is no such title as Chief Justice of the United States Supreme Court. There are Associate Justices, but there is no Chief Justice title like that.

The reason that Peter's answer was correct is the reason why the Attorney General is not the Attorney General of the Justice Department – the true title is Attorney General <u>of the United States</u>. The same applies to the

63

Supreme Court: John Roberts' true title is Chief Justice <u>of the United States</u>... how's that for a way to win some money making bets in a bar?

That's a piece of trivia, but at that point in the story it's relevant – and, it's an interesting and educational, the type of thing that readers enjoy. When they finish the chapter that dialogue exchange appears in, they feel smarter: they know something they didn't know before reading that chapter... something that their friends probably don't know, and they'll no doubt be professing their new-found knowledge at every opportunity, looking forward to finishing the book and hopefully others in the series, hoping to pick up more tidbits like that.

Anyway, getting back to the first book of the series, I tried another interesting device – a new civil action. Some years back a lady was struck by a San Francisco cable car. She had no visible injuries, but her lawyers contended that as a result of the traumatic experience of being struck, she became a nymphomaniac.

I was a trial lawyer for over twenty years and never came across a case like that, but I sure wish I had. I'd have loved to have represented the cable car company and gotten that plaintiff on the witness stand to cross-examine her, because I'd like to see how she would attempt to prove up her case.

Unfortunately for the legal journals and jurisdictional history, the case never went to trial: it was settled, and she is reported to have received $25,000 for her non-troubles.

The case was unique in its own way, and I felt it deserved being brought back to life in a new manner, so I had Peter's friend Stuart receive a summons and complaint from one of his weight-loss-drink customers, contending that his product may have helped her to lose weight, but it also turned her into a nymphomaniac, and she wanted to recover damages.

In the book (and in promotional blurbs) we referred to the case as one of **Negligent Nymphomania** and in many cases that phrase alone was tantamount to what I described earlier in the book as Nick Shoveen's making the title of his low-budget film primer *How to be a Porno Producer*. The new civil tort action I created had that tinge of naughtiness that attracts eyeballs and encourages sales. Yes, I know. I can be accused of prostituting myself as an author and trying to appeal to the readers' prurient interests. I plead guilty as charged... but it sold books and I'll bet you're curious to see how that lady's case concluded.

Chapter Fifteen: No Loose Ends

I've touched upon the subject of tying up loose ends in a novel earlier in this book, but right now I'd like to zero in on it a little closer, with a little history.

Before you were born (and before I was born, too) there was a series of black-and-white movies featuring William Powell and Myrna Loy (ask your grandparents about them) playing the parts of a married couple named Nick and Nora North. Their dog is probably more memorable nowadays, because his name appears quite frequently in crossword puzzles, with the clue "movie dog." His name was Asta

[Cliff Clavin note: The first movie featuring Nick, Nora and Asta were based on a book entitled **The Thin Man**, written by Dashiell Hammett... and if you intend to be a mystery writer, you'd better do some research and find out how good Mr. Hammett was. He also wrote a book entitled **the Maltese Falcon**, in which he created a character named Sam Spade. Oh, by the way, the part of Asta was played by a dog named Skippy.]

Nick and Nora North were wealthy socialites, but they always seemed to get involve d in a murder case, and as would be expected, they solved it. Actually, she was the socialite and Nick was an alcoholic retired detective. They dressed well, formally most of the time, attended great parties, drank a lot, and had fun... typical married couple... and about fifteen minutes into each movie, someone you didn't like would get murdered.

Naturally, the movie's regular police lieutenant was usually portrayed as a boob, so solving the crime always rested on Nick and Nora's shoulders, and they never disappointed. As far as I was concerned, the most interesting part of each movie was the last ten minutes. In the old cowboy movies, the last ten minutes was called "the Chase," when the bad guy would try to get away and the good guy (on his white horse) would chase after him - and then some stunt double would jump off of the white horse and tackle another stunt double off of his black horse and onto the ground, where the stunt doubles would then trade places with the stars, so that they could pretend to be fighting. Ah, reality – ain't it great?

There were no horse chases at the end of a Nick and Nora movie: instead, they held what was called a "showdown." This was a session in which Nick, Nora, the police, and all the usual suspects would assemble in the same room so that Nick could walk around the room and start pointing at one person after another, with lines like, "I knew that Frebish didn't do it, because..." and he would continue with each person until he fingered the real murderer, who was always expected to pull a revolver out of his suit coat (the men always wore suits and fedoras in those movies) and angrily confess to the crime, blurting out why he did it.

Of course there was no getting away, because somehow they always managed to subdue the bad guy and cart him away, leaving the screen available for Nick to make some smarmy remark to Nora about where they'll be getting their next drink.

The showdown became a popular device in crime-solving movies and books. Author Rex Stout used it quite extensively, usually ending each book with all the parties involved being summoned to his office, during which time armchair detective Nero Wolfe would conduct his 'showdown,' revealing the guilty person and how he solved the crime.

In other forms, we've seen it in the television series featuring Erle Stanly Gardner's famous lawyer **Perry Mason**. The 'showdown' in those television shows always took place in the courtroom, where Mason would always be able to get some witness to break down and confess to the crime, thereby exonerating Perry's client.

Andy Griffith's attorney Matlock usually did the same thing, but in a sort of 'down home' kind of way, which is about the only way you can do things when you're wearing a cheap suit and suspenders.

In a mystery novel, it's not an easy task to get a dozen people in a room where dialogue will be exchanged and a lot of cross-talking going on. In the Nero Wolfe stories,

Wolfe did all the talking, so the books came off quite well.

In my books, I don't play games. Like this book, each chapter has a number except three: if used in the book, they don't have numbers – they have names: **The Trial**, **The Solution**, and **Epilogue**.

I wised up to adding an Epilogue in the third book of the series, but didn't start using The Solution until the fifth book, and it made things a lot easier, because a novel can go a lot deeper than a one-hour (45 minute average) television program. The average person reads a novel at a rate of about 45 pages per hour, so if they only had 45 minutes of reading time, they would only get through about 35 pages, and that's probably less than one-seventh of the average 250-page book.

On television, all that counts is that the bad guy gets caught. The last few minutes of the show are usually taken up by the main characters celebrating the victory and having a laugh. I don't know how many time I've seen that 'everyone's laughing' final scene on Angela Lansbury's old show **Murder She Wrote**. Perry Mason was no different, with Mason, Della and their invest-igator all having a final laugh together.

You can do much better in a book – and you'd better. After the bad guy is arrested, there should be a detailed explanation, and we should also know what happens to the other people – those who were wrongly accused, collateral victims, etc. I like to see those people have a happy ending too, hence the need for an Epilogue.

69

I also like to build tension by always having my hero Peter Sharp fighting time against an upcoming trial date, while struggling to figure out how he can possibly defend his apparently guilty client. It's a lot like those old cowboy movies where the Indians are attacking the circled wagon train, and the film editors cleverly intersperse scenes of the cavalry galloping to the rescue – but they're still far away (on another section of the studio's back lot) will they get there in time?

Just like Perry Mason and Matlock, Peter Sharp never loses a case. The only difference with his trials is **how** he wins. Perry Mason usually has his investigator miraculously find the disappearing witness, and waltz her into the courtroom at the very last minute. Matlock does it by trapping the dull-normal criminal in a lie. Peter Sharp does it in different ways: some of his own doing and some things cooked up by little Suzi.

During the course of each book, Peter will see strangers coming to their yacht, but he never questions those visits, presuming that the kid is up to something that has something to do with the present case, but as usual, will never reveal what it is until she's good and ready.

Bottom line: Tie it all up by the end of the book. The old-style 'showdown' has been replaced over the past few years by the clever interrogation. Two prime examples of this are **the Closer**, and **Law & Order Criminal Intent.**

The last portion of those show is where the main protagonist gets the guest star bad-person in an interrogation room, and by using lies, intimidation, stories of non-existent evidence, hinting at a co-conspirator wanting to make deal, or any other device, tricks the antagonist into a confession... and when done well, it's really fun to watch.

Chapter Sixteen: We Can All Get Along

Dramatic motion pictures require that the lead player goes through what's known in entertainment circles as a 'character arc.' They change during the movie and are almost different people at the end. A prime example of this is when two people don't get along at all in the beginning, but form a mutual respect that they find difficult to express at the end of the movie – but the audience knows it's there, even if the characters don't say it.

A prime example of this is the relationship between Sidney Poitier and Rod Steiger in the 1967 classic film **In the Heat of the Night,** in which black Virgil Tibbs crosses swords with the local white police chief Gillespie.

[Clavin note: the movie was originally set to be shot in Mississippi, but because of racial politics was instead moved to Sparta, Illinois, where the title of the town was changed in the script to Sparta, Mississippi, so that local signs didn't have to be changed. Steiger got an Academy Award for his performance.]

The last scene in the movie, where Tibbs and Gillespie are sitting at the railroad station waiting for Tibbs' train exemplifies how their relationship has changed, even though Steiger's Gillespie character can't get any words of friendship out of his mouth.

If you plan on utilizing a character arc in your mystery story, I would advise you to have someone other than your main protagonist go through it. Stop and think about it: if your lead player goes through a life-changing character arc in each book, what will he (or she) be like several books down the road?

Readers keep coming back to characters in books the same way that the Grateful Dead was able to pack concert venues time after time over the years. People find something they like, and want to stick with it.

I've mentioned a fellow author from my publisher, Magic Lamp Press – Nice Shoveen. He's written a book entitled **What Women Really Mean – the Female-to-English Dictionary**. (www.WhatWomenReallyMean.com)

Early in that book he sets forth what usually strains every marriage slowly, over time. His theory is that a man falls in love with a woman and never wants her to change: he wants that girl he fell in love with to stay that way forever.

On the contrary, when a woman sees a man, no matter how much she may care for him, she looks at him as a 'work in progress...' something that given time, she thinks she can mold into what she will consider to be a respectable representative to the world of their marriage

Unfortunately, each party to the marriage gets the exact opposite results of what they wished for. The girl he wished would never change does change – a lot. And the guy she thought she could mold into something a lot more acceptable stays exactly the same: as if every trait was etched in stone.

The lead characters in a book are looked at by readers a lot like the guy in a marriage looks at his new bride: they don't want the characters to change. They want them to stay that way. They like that way. They feel comfortable that way.

It's like you getting a Saint Bernard puppy. Boy, they're adorable. You wish they could stay that way... but they sure don't, and in a year's time you've got a huge beast slobbering all over the house.

Now don't get me wrong. I'm in no way likening the way a wife changes to the way a Saint Bernard does, so please concentrate on what I mean, and not on what I say. I've got enough problems with the opposite sex now... I don't need any more.

Character arcs can be rewarding, but there can only be change when compared to some fixed frame of reference. In order to notice a character arc, there must be some other person who doesn't change, so that a comparison of the respective behaviors can be made.

In at least one of my books, Peter and his prosecutor ex-wife are drawn together working side by side on a non-criminal case. No matter how much conflict there is between their personalities and legal philosophies, you can sense that there is an underlying trust that one won't sell the other out. Myra may be left hanging in an embarrassing courtroom situation, but it won't be because of something Peter purposely did – it might be because either he or the kid goofed up somewhere along the line. She may be angry at him, but she won't have that feeling of betrayal... and the readers don't want to see their lead characters betrayed by each other.

Another reason you want to leave your lead characters alone and for the most part unchanged is because you want them to be able to build some trust between each other. There has to be some dependability in the story. This is not a CIA thriller where you don't know who's going to turn out to be the mole – it's a mystery story with a lead character or two that can be repeated from book to book, and the readers need to feel that underlying stability. They may not have it in their own life, so let's give them some trustworthiness and stability in the books we write for them to read.

*****

In one of the books in my series (***The Reluctant Jurist***) Peter is called upon to fill in for a judge who is down with the flu.

He has had quite a few run-ins with members of the bench, but they all know that he's never lied to them.

75

He might try a devious stunt during a trial, but they respect his ethics in never having a client lie on the stand and never trying to mislead the court.

In another book of the series (**A Good Alibi**) Peter is drafted by the prosecution to help them figure out how to break a suspect's iron-clad alibi. They all know in their hearts that he's guilty of the murder, which took place across town, but several times during the time of the murder he claims he was walking home from a shopping spree, and kept making calls to the police department inquiring about the status of his stolen car report.

The incoming calls were recorded (as is usual in police departments) and it was actually him calling. The cell phone company's towers triangulated the position each call was coming from, and they were all where he says he was, on the way home, all the way across town from where the murder was committed. For Peter to break this alibi, he'd have to show how the suspect could be in two places at the same time, in different parts of the city.

Peter's ex-wife, District Attorney Myra wouldn't hesitate a moment to lock Peter up if he broke the law, but she and her department still respected him enough to ask for his help in trying to break a suspect's alibi.

The books seem to display a status of 'friendly enemies' and that's good thing, because a vicious hatred between parties is too strong of an emotion to maintain over a series of books. It has to be tempered a little so that the parties can communicate: this gives an author a good opportunity for some interesting dialogue. Conversation between adversaries is always more compelling than conversation between friends.

I remember one movie in particular (**Heat**) starring both Robert De Niro as bad guy Neil McCauley and Al Pacino as police Lieutenant Vincent Hanna. The story itself wasn't that compelling, but a lot of movie-goers (me included) went to see that film just to see the scene where the both of them wind up having a conversation together in a coffee shop. It's a polite conversation with neither of them shouting at each other, but Pacino lets De Niro know that he plans to 'take him down,' and De Niro politely explains that he won't hesitate to use lethal force to avoid being 'taken down.'

That conversation was much more interesting than any of the other dialogue in the movie that takes place between people on the same side.

Bottom line: Conflict is good, and so is change – but not of the lead players.

Chapter Seventeen: The Way it Really Is

No matter what your occupation is, there's bound to be some television show or movie that depicts a character doing the same thing that you do. And no matter how hard they try, they never seem to get it right. They can come close, but they just can't get it right. They can get so close that anyone but a person like you who also does that for a living thinks it looks right – but they can't ever really get it right.

There are movies and/or television shows about a lot of different jobs: Cable Guy, UPS driver, CIA agents, doctors, lawyers, cops, robbers, etc., etc. I've seen 'em all, and the only ones that really bother me are the ones about lawyers.

Law is a popular subject now. **Inherit the Wind** with Spencer Tracy and Frederick March, and **Witness for the Prosecution** were one thing... they were classics, so I cut them a bit of slack. But I expect the modern stuff like **Law & Order** to be a little more accurate.

First of all, I'm tired of seeing a suspect interrogated for a while and then some mealy-mouthed, arrogant, rude, sarcastic defense lawyer comes strutting in, declaring "this interrogation is now over. I'm taking my client out of here right now!" And as they walk out, the defense lawyer slaps some blue-backed legal document into the D.A.'s hand, declaring "and you'll never be able to get that gun into evidence."

I don't care how acrimonious the relationship between Marcia Clark and the defense attorneys in the O.J. Simpson case appeared while it was being televised, opposing counsel don't hate each other's guts and act so confrontational with each other... at least I've never seen it that way.

Most of the time an attorney will become friendly with members of the opposing party. They meet at Bar Association dinners, and quite often have gone to law school together. True, they may have differing philosophies about law and order, but they can still maintain some level of civility amongst them.

I spent several years working as a defense attorney in the Juvenile Justice System here in Southern California, where we would sometimes try up to three felony cases a day – and it was quite common for the defense attorney and prosecutor to get together for lunch. Quite often a few of the D.A.'s cop witnesses would also join us, and we would joke about how they should get plenty of calories in them because later that afternoon we're going to tear them apart when they get on the witness stand.

It got to a point where there were one or two police investigators who appeared quite often in cases I was defending. We became quite friendly, and looked forward to battling it out in court, the same way that a father and son can enjoy playing a game of one-on-one basketball out in the driveway.

****

Another thing that really gets my goat is the way the lawyers prance around in the courtroom – in front of the counsel tables.

In a real courtroom, the area between the counsel table and the judge's bench is called 'the well,' and it's completely off limits to anyone but court personnel. If you want to approach the bench for any reason, you have to ask first. If you have a piece of paper or something you want the judge to look at, you do NOT walk over and hand it to him. The bailiff will hear your conversation with the judge, so all you have to do is hold your hand out and the bailiff will be there to take it out of your hand and walk it over to the judge.

If you want to approach the witness for any reason, like to refresh his or her memory by showing some piece of evidence, or ask the witness to identify a piece of evidence or signature, you must first ask the court's permission to 'approach the witness.' There is no standing by the witness box with your elbow on the rail, shouting insinuations at the witness. It doesn't happen. Period.

****

In the Perry Mason court trials, all the suspects were present in the courtroom while the trial was taking place: even those who would be called to testify.

This might be a good thing to have for theatrical purposes because it gives the viewers a chance to see reactions on the faces of people who are being testified about by any witness – but in real life, that doesn't happen.

The court is not interested in giving witnesses an opportunity to hone their upcoming testimony, based upon what previous witnesses have testified to. In criminal cases (the most common in movies and TV), witnesses are excluded from the courtroom until they are called to testify; most of the time they just sit out in the hall and wait to be called.

Sometimes, if there's a spare empty jury room, they may allow police officers to wait in there until called in to testify.

****

I'm also tired of seeing lawyers testify while questioning a witness. All you're supposed to do is ask a question and wait for the answer. That's it. It's not appropriate to make a comment after you get your answer. In real life, we don't say things like "I see," or "that's your testimony?" or any other type of comment. It's not appropriate.

Another thing they do is have lawyers from different sides of the aisle communicate directly with each other. That's not to be done either. If there's something you want to say to opposing counsel, you have two choices: One is to tell the judge your request, "You Honor we would appreciate the Court instructing opposing counsel that he should refrain from..." The other alternative is for you to ask the court for brief recess of two minutes or so, to give you an opportunity to discuss a matter with opposing counsel.

It's unlikely that any people other than attorneys or court personnel notice these theatrical errors, but I guess that some of them are required for the sake of 'production value,' because people sitting behind a table for the whole trial would look as boring on television and in the movies as it really is in real life.

Bottom line: if you intend to write story that involves people doing something specialized like law, medicine, accounting, plumbing, acting, etc., etc. you should go out and talk to some people who really do that for a living. Ask what bugs them about television and movies depicting people supposed to be doing what they do.

In many instances, that might also be a good dialogue point, when a character in your story might say something like "what do you think this is a television show? I do this for a living, and people in my business would never do _____ like that."

Remember, people who read books are the type of people who also like to learn things – and if your book can entertain them while also giving them a little relevant tidbit they didn't know before, you'll score points with them and they'll be looking forward to your next book.

Chapter Eighteen: I'll Call You Back

A popular plot device can be established by bringing something in to your story early on, and then referring to it again later in the story – or have it come back to bite someone in the rear several chapters later.

In the field of professional comedy, they have what's referred to as a "Callback." That's where a comedian gets a good laugh from some joke or funny line during his routine, and then spots an opportunity to repeat that punch line with respect to another joke. It will generally get a good laugh the second time too, and professional comedians who 'headline' claim that in a one-hour show, you can use a callback successfully up to three times.

An example of a callback is one night on a talkshow the host was doing his monologue and interrupted it to address a girl who was laughing hysterically. He intuitively knew that it would be a good exchange if he could talk to her.

When the house lights were brightened and she was handed a microphone, they had a humorous conversation, and the host noted that she had something printed on her T-shirt, so he asked what it was. She responded that because of her large breasts, she decided to give each of them a name, so the shirt was labeled: one was Thelma, and the other was Louise.

This got a good laugh out of the audience, so the comedian host, being the pro that he was, remembered it. Halfway through the show, just before a commercial break, he told the audience (especially the viewing audience at home), "Don't go away folks. When we come back we'll spend some time with Harrison Ford, and Thelma and Louise." As the show went to commercial, you could hear the audience roaring with laughter.

That callback was effective on its own, but to a live audience, it was treated as in inside joke that they were all in on.

In a mystery novel you shouldn't have any need for comedy callbacks, but there are other kinds you can use effectively – not to get a laugh, but as effective plot devices – and the callback doesn't have to be spoken or dialogue of any kind, it can be the action of someone.

Several times in an old western movie you might see the lead character being friendly with young Indian boy, perhaps even rescuing him from some perilous position.

Later on towards the end of the movie when the lead character and his small group of fellow travelers are on the trail they are confronted by a group of bad guys who no doubt mean them harm. The good guys know that this is it: no rescue in sight, and they don't have a chance to fight their way out of this situation. Suddenly, the bad guys all turn their horses around and get out of there in a big rush.

The good guys don't know what happened to make the bad guys run away until one of them calls their attention to the top of the cliff behind them. Lined up on that mesa are about 100 Indians in war paint, and on the horse in front of them is the Chief's son.

When the good guy hero looks up at the young boy on the horse, he recognizes him as the lad he saved earlier in the movie. The young Indian boy smiles and waves down at him, as all the Indians turn to ride away. And that's a movie callback... but it's really nothing new, because it all started with the old story about the guy who removed a thorn from a lion cub's paw.

You probably won't have any cowboys or Indians in your mystery novel, but you can still use a callback. It can take the form of any person who gets helped in the first part of the story who then becomes the unexpected helper later on.

Another twist is to make the callback person a previous adversary. This type of situation accomplishes two birds with one stone: first, it's an effective callback. Second, it represents a character arc for the former adversary who has now decided to help out.

In the cowboy situation, the Indians rode away. In your novel, the former adversaries can become 'friendly enemies,' sharing a mutual respect that can go both ways towards the end of the story.

No problem with a character arc of a person you'll never see again.

In some of my books I have attorney Peter Sharp crossing swords with an FBI Special Agent in the West Los Angeles office. There's a certain amount of conflict between them, but there's also a certain amount of mutual respect that comes creeping through, especially when Peter and his friends meddle with an FBI investigation and wind up solving the case. At the press conference the FBI agent is quietly fuming over the fact that an amateur will be stealing his credit for gang-busting, until Peter does the unexpected: he states that all the credit belongs to Special Agent _____, without whose help the case couldn't have been broken.

From that moment on, and in several subsequent books, the FBI agent cuts Peter a little slack, having confidence in him that true to his word, he would never try to upstage the FBI by claiming credit.

That type of situation was a form of callback not from an earlier part of the same book, but from a previous book. I don't know how far back you can go, but whatever works is okay with me.

Arnold Schwarzenegger, California's 'governator' made most of his movies several years ago, but whenever he leaves politics, I think that a clever callback would be for him to say "I'll be back," a tag line of his from a movie he made called **The Terminator**, back in 1984.

He used it a second time in **Terminator 2: Judgment Day** seven years later, when he said "Stay here, I'll be back."

Not tired of the line yet, his writers forced a version of it in again in 2003, when he said "She'll be back" in the second sequel, **Terminator 3: Rise of the Machines**.

In 2009, the writers felt compelled to use it again, but this time by another actor who said "I'll be back" in what should hopefully be the last movie in the series, **Terminator Salvation**.

<u>Bottom line</u>: it looks like the callback shelf-life of a good line is at least 25 years... and still counting.

Chapter Nineteen: Do Your Homework!

There's a pharmacy in my neighborhood that everyone I know uses with great satisfaction. The pharmacist who owns the place is a really nice guy who seems like one of most knowledgeable people I've met in a long time.

I shop in his small store occasionally and don't hesitate to ask him for advice about products that purport to alleviate symptoms of cold and/or flu, but no matter how much respect I have for him as a person and a pharmacist, I definitely wouldn't select him to be the primary surgeon if I needed to have my appendix removed.

There's a young man living near my boat who spends most of his time shooting video of boats in the harbor. From what people tell me, his ambition is to one day write, produce and direct a great western movie.

I had an opportunity to speak to him one day, and he confirmed what had been said about him: he really does want to make a great western movie. During our conversation, I asked him about some previous cowboy flicks, just to see what his opinion about them was.

To my surprise, I learned that he has never seen **High Noon, Shane, The Magnificent Seven, Stagecoach, The Shootist, Unforgiven**, the Spaghetti Westerns, or any of the others 'oaters' I asked him about. He stated that he'd rather not be influenced by the work of others. He wants to be original.

Guaranteed – if he does write, produce and direct a western – it **will** be an original.

At this point you might be wondering what the pharmacist and the boat videographer have to do with the title of this chapter, and the answer is - if you plan on writing a mystery book, you are targeting a hard-core audience of mystery lovers. They have probably read stories written by Arthur Conan Doyle, Dashiell Hammett, Edgar Allen Poe, John le Carré, Raymond Chandler, Agatha Christie, Ellery Queen, Rex Stout, Donald Westlake, and too many more to mention here. Remember – your target audience likes a particular type of book, and a certain amount of creativity within the genre is appreciated, but not stuff that's just too far out or a repetition of something that's already been.

Therefore, you must do your homework. If you plan on writing mysteries, read them first. Read as many as you can: you don't have to spend any money on it either, because websites like Gutenberg and others offer thousands of eBooks free of charge. They're all at least 70 years old, but so are all of the *Sherlock Holmes* stories. It's not hard at all to get past the rotary dial phones, British spelling of *honour* and *labour*, and references to horses and carriages: just pay attention to the plots. Remember – the play's the thing. It doesn't matter that it's a 'period' piece.

[Clavin note: Famous mystery writer **Ellery Queen** didn't exist, because it was a pen-name used by two cousins - Frederic Dannay and Manfred Bennington Lee. But it goes even deeper than that, because the real names of those two were actually Daniel Nathan and Manford Emanuel Lepofsky.]

It's really hard to think of something that hasn't been done before. Get used to that. There are only so many ways you can weave blackmail into a plot. Same goes for the other plot devices. Therefore it's incumbent on you to read as many stories as you can, to avoid repeating something that someone else has done.

If there's a murder in your book, it's going to be hard for you to figure out a way to whack someone like nobody has ever done before, but you **can** get creative in designing a motive, an escape plan, an alibi, a legal defense, a conspiracy, etc., etc.

It also would be very educational and helpful if you watched some of the greatest mystery movies. Remember, your readers will be watching a mental movie of what you've written as it is being read, so you might what to help them out a little by seeing how the pro's do it on film... and listen to the movie's background music: that's a great aid to building suspense. You can't put music into your book, but when you hear the 'something's gonna happen' music in the background of a movie, pay attention to what's taking place on the screen, because that's the way you create suspense.

Here's a good system for you to use: First, with the aid of Microsoft Excel, create a database for mystery books with fields for Title, Author, date read and Comments. Then, start shopping on the internet for free eBooks by the best mystery writers. Next, go to bookstores and see how many used books you can scrounge up for a buck each. This is not a quick-fix process... it's a learning process, and you should do it for a couple of years, until you feel comfortable with it, updating your worksheet each time you find another title – and carry a copy of it with you whenever you go book-hunting, because lots of times a book will be re-issued with a new cover and you don't want to make the mistake of buying it again, like I've done too many times to count.

Many times I've been asked "how do I know when I'm ready to start writing?" The answer is **now**. Start framing an outline of what your book might be. There are few people in the civilized developed world who don't have access to Microsoft Word, so you can always update the outline, move things around, do a global search to find names to change, and alter plot points... as you're reading what the masters have done.

And as for when you should feel confident to actually get your first book ready for submission to the printer and eBook listing, there are two signs that you should watch for:

First, when after reading a large enough number of mysteries you start to be able to have a pretty good idea of what the solution will be;

Second, after reading a book put out by a major publishing house you feel – "I can do that!" Then, you're probably ready.

And as for when you should feel confident to actually get your first book ready for submission to the printer and eBook listing, there are two signs that you should watch for:

First, when after reading a large enough number of mysteries you start to be able to have a pretty good idea of what the solution will be;

Second, after reading a book put out by a major publishing house you feel – "I can do that!" Then, you're ready.

<u>Helpful tip</u>: publish you work as an ebook on Kindle first, because it's free, it's easy, and you'll have time to correct typos and other mistakes without having to redo any printing

.

Chapter Twenty: Have Some Fun

No matter how serious your subject matter is, there's no reason you can't have a little fun while writing it.

I do two different things for enjoyment while I'm writing fiction. First, I work into the story people with names very similar to old friends of mine back in my home town of Chicago.

The old gang follows my writing career and get a real kick out of recognizing themselves as characters in the my books. One special twist is to give their names to characters that are far from their real-life persona. For example, one particular friend is named Jack B_____, and he has done spectacularly well in the construction industry and with investments – so, I only thought it proper that his name be attached to Peter Sharp's private investigator Jack Bibberman, who is a very poor guy and can do everything well - but make a living.

Not only do my friends enjoy seeing themselves in the book, they let me know that other former acquaintances have asked them for favors: could they please get Gene to name characters after them too?

I've been a great Sherlock Holmes fan ever since elementary school, so I have a lot of fun inserting Sherlock Holmes references into the stories.

I don't want to give away my Holmes secrets, but I'll let you have this one: in two of the books, Peter Sharp comes up against an attorney that annoys him. The man is arrogant, and Peter doesn't think he deserves to be licensed to practice law because his ethics appear to be extremely questionable.

This attorney not only practices law, but he also teaches it at a local law school, where he is an assistant professor. The lawyer's name is Morris Arthur.

If you feel like doing a little detective work here, try and think what the abbreviated nicknames are for the names Morris and Arthur. They might be things like Morrie and Artie... and the guy's a professor. Put it together yet?

That's tiny tidbit of the little things I sneak into the stories. Not all of my readers are Holmes fans like me, but for the few who are, there are a few special treats waiting for them in each book.

*****

I grudgingly watched almost ten years of the **Seinfeld** TV show for only one reason: the genius of Larry David in making the show a true Sit-Com... one in which the characters didn't have to hit each other in the face with pies, wear funny hats, shout one-liners at each other, do funny accents, say outrageously funny things or tell funny stories. All they had to do was act normal: the 'situation' was the star.

Sit-Com is an abbreviated slang word that's supposed to describe a Situation Comedy, and Larry David truly understands how to set up that genre... as he went on to continue doing with his **Curb Your Enthusiasm** cable show.

The reason I used the word "grudgingly" above is because not one character in the Seinfeld show had any socially redeeming character traits. They were all self-centered, selfish individuals. I didn't like them, but I enjoyed watching how the situations created for the show played out – strictly from a writer's standpoint.

At this point I'm sure you're asking what this might have to do with writing a mystery, and the answer is that no matter how good you can create a situation (plot), it always helps to have a likeable lead character.

You might be able to get people to watch a group of insensitive brats for 22 minutes once week if there's nothing better on during the same time slot, but I wouldn't suggest trying to get someone to invest 5 to 7 hours of time reading a book with not one likeable character involved – unless it's a biography of Adolph Hitler or Saddam Hussein... and even that might be a tough sell... but stories about Marilyn Monroe, Elvis Presley and Michael Jackson will always make the bookstore cash registers go ka-ching.

My main criteria in judging television cast members (and politicians is "would I like to have beer with that person?" Political philosophy aside, if you had a choice of which two you'd like to have a beer with between George W. Bush, Bill Clinton, Dick Cheney, and Joe Lieberman, I'll bet that Bush and Clinton would be the most likeable – even though you preferred one over the other as a politician.

The cover of this book mentions that it's a behind-the-scenes look at the creation of a crime series – the operative word being "series." That infers more than one book, with a repeating main protagonist... and that person, whether it be male, female, child or adult, should be likeable; someone you'd like to have a beer (or a milkshake) with.

Writing is more than a creative art – it's a business. Your job is to make people want to give you money so they can spend time reading your books, so why make it hard for them? If you're writing a mystery or crime series, sure, you're going to have some bad guys involved, but their 'badness' is a relative condition. If your main protagonist isn't 'good,' then there's no conflict.

I'm not trying to suggest that your hero has to be some squeaky-clean comic-strip do-gooder; he or she can drink, play around (TV shows ***Nurse Jackie***, ***Saving Grace***, or ***House***), but for goodness sake, please consider giving the reader some reason to think "I wonder what he or she will be up to in this author's next book."

Sometimes it's tough to get past annoying habits of people like *Adrian Monk* (obsessive compulsive disorder), *Sherlock Holmes* (poor violin-playing and 7% cocaine), *Lt. Columbo* (aggravating one-last-question syndrome and smelly cigar), *the Closer* (sugar addiction and sugary southern accent), but you have to admit that their likeable crime-solving talent far outweighs their annoying habits.

<u>Bottom line</u>: As a writer, you're always in a constant balancing act, and my suggestion is that you should try and make the scales tip towards the 'likeable' side.

***

And as far as likeable people are concerned, you may be about to become one. Here's something that will come as a pleasant surprise when you publish your first book.

It's natural to order a bunch of copies and pass them out to your friends and family.

The surprise will come when you hand a dear old friend or family member your book to read, and they ask you to sign it for them!

Yes, they actually will ask for your autograph. That freaks me out a little, especially when it's a close friend or family member, but what the heck – why not? See? You have now become likeable.

The Last Chapter: Finding Readers

This is the hard part, because if you're not signed up by a big publishing company, you won't have any advertising to help spur sales of your book. You also won't have access to the right reviewers for your title, and even if you do, it can get expensive to ship sample copies out to each of them, and then follow through to see if they've read and reviewed it before offering it up for sale on eBay.

I did it the hard way, and after a couple of years, my method started to 'get legs.'

First, I waited until 2003, when I had completed at least five books in the series before putting them up with CreateSpace for printing. I didn't start listing them as eBooks until 2005, and only did a couple, because the companies performing formatting services were quite expensive in those early days of digital reading.

Second, as soon as Amazon started listing eBooks and accepted them in pdf form, I immediately listed every title I had available, and continue to do that.

Third, I created a website (**www.LegalMystery.com**), where all of the books could be seen (especially the covers), with links to how each one could be ordered in print version and also as either Kindle or non-Kindle eBook format.

CAVEAT: If you visit the Legal Mystery website you'll also see some other books my publisher insisted be shown there – like the ones referenced earlier by Nick Shoveen… I couldn't refuse the 'request' because the publisher is paying for the website hosting.

Fourth, I used a local (Van Nuys, California) printing company that caters to authors and publishers, and designed a bookmark with some pictures of the covers, plus the website address, and had a thousand of them printed (it cost less than a hundred dollars). When you're ready, you can do the same thing: contact David Field. His email address is **sales@separacolor.com**

Helpful tips:
1. Once you have a website up and running, you'll start getting a lot of spam email from companies offering to optimize search results to bring more traffic to your website. Rule number 1: never do business with any company that spams you. The mere fact that they send out millions of spam messages is an indication that their business ethics are questionable, and if those defective ethics are used to bring traffic to your website, they may do things against the rules of search engines, which might result in your getting completely removed from Google – which will leave you dead in the water.

2. If you're searching for an SEO (Search Engine
    Optimization) company to help you attract more
    internet traffic, the best way to find one is to use
    "SEO" as a search term on Google, Yahoo and
    Bing, and see who the top twenty SEO companies
    are on each of those top search engines. Make a
    list of those top twenty and see if there is any
    cross-connection showing that one or more of
    those firms is in the top twenty of more than one
    search engine. The moral of this plan is that if an
    SEO company promises to do such a good job for
    you, then they should at least have been
    successful in doing a good job for themselves, so
    only pick a company that's got a good position in
    the search engine results.

Also, the good thing about having a series of books
instead of just one is that once you get a reader who
likes your books, you've got a potential customer for the
entire series, and that's a lot better than if you've only
got one book because then, after that one book has
been read, the customer is gone forever... and more
readers through successful SEO results can mean more
readers for all the books in your series.

First Chapters

You only get two chances to make a first impression, because this is the order of things that a prospective reader will see first:

One: Your book's front cover;

Two: Your book's first chapter

We've included first chapters for some of our books, but because this is a black-and-white interior text layout, we won't be showing the covers but you can see them at my main website:

www.LegalMystery.com.

We're strong believers in cross-promotion, so at the end of each of the books in the series, we usually include summaries of all of the books.

If the reader has enjoyed the first book, we hope they will want to read the others, too – and from the feedback we've received, this plan has received some moderate success.

When you read the first chapters you may notice a development of the characters and of the relationships between them.

Single Jeopardy
Peter Sharp Legal Mystery #1

> If a shipbuilder build a boat for some one, and do not make it tight, and if during that same year that boat is sent away and suffers injury, the shipbuilder shall take the boat apart and put it together tight at his own expense. The tight boat he shall give to the boat owner.
>
> *Number 235, from Hammurabi' s Code of 282 Laws*

Chapter 1

Boating can be a great sport, but not in a back yard – which is where I'm presently doing my yachting, as the result of several swift moves choreographed by my soon-to-be ex-wife and her beady-eyed divorce lawyer, whose cheap business card should be changed to read 'Gary Koontz, Schmuck at Law.'

My sleeping quarters were involuntarily changed from the bedroom, to the living room couch, and then out to this 1956 classic forty-foot Chris Craft Constellation, a bull-nosed cabin cruiser I've been restoring out here in the yard for the past seven years. Having been told to take the rest of my life off by the law firm I was formerly employed by, I'm sitting here in the cabin of my boat/office talking on the phone to my San Fernando Valley friend Stuart.

One good thing about Stuart is that no matter how bad off you might think you're doing, Stuart can convince you he's doing worse... and he usually is. His cause de jour is suing the United States Government and some large corporations for poisoning him: he claims to be suffering from mesothelioma, a form of asbestos damage to the lining of his lungs that he claims was a result of spending four years working in the Navy as a ship's boiler room engineer.

To humor him, I prepared and filed a lawsuit last month so that he wouldn't blow the Statute of Limitations, and now he wants to go ahead with it by having the U.S. Marshall's office serve the lawsuit on all the defendants.

Wonderful. A federal case. Just what I need at this low point in my life. I tell him now that I'm semi-retired I don't have the office staff, but I'll try to associate another attorney in on the case who is much better equipped to handle this type of case.

My involuntary retirement may not be such a bad thing after all, considering the fact that there'll be no boat restoration distractions from clients like Stuart. For the past few years, every time he calls it's to either file another lawsuit or go with him to meet his uncle Label, who's supposed to own a boat in the Marina.

When I was a kid, growing up in Chicago on North Kedzie Avenue, one of my favorite Saturday afternoon pastimes was packing a lunch and hopping on my bike for a long bike ride down Lawrence Avenue, and then south along Sheridan Road, to Belmont Harbor. I would spend all afternoon there sitting on the concrete seawall, daydreaming, my legs dangling over the edge. I used to rest my arms on the middle rung of the guard rail – the rail that kept the have-nots without boats away from the privileged few 'haves' who not only had boats, but also had the political pull to get a mooring in the city's most popular Marina. The daydream was usually the same... someday I'd have one of those big, shiny, varnished wood cabin cruisers, complete with an ornament that so many of them seemed to be displaying on their foreward decks – a beautiful redheaded wife.

It took almost thirty years, before fate was kind to me - but with a string attached: I was allowed to achieve my dream, but found out you aren't allowed to enjoy both the boat and the wife at the same time.

There's a tragic procedure that takes place in many marriages, all brought about by a conflict of goals. A woman will view a prospective husband as a work in progress... a project... an acquisition she can transform into something respectable who is safe to bring to boring social functions. On the other hand, a man looks at a woman, likes what he sees, and hopes that she stays just like that forever - without ever changing.

Unfortunately, the opposite of what they each hoped for usually takes place. The woman fails in all her attempts to change the man, whose traits are usually etched in stone. And on the other side of the equation, the woman goes through all the personality and cosmetic changes, winding up being nothing like what the husband thought he would spend the rest of his life with. Some states have a six-month waiting period before a divorce becomes final, but it might be a better idea to put the waiting period in front, making it a six-month wait and then a trial period before the marriage is a locked-in deal.

Neither going through changes nor staying the same is necessarily a bad thing, but either case can cause disappointment and strain on a marriage. That's what happened in our case. My wife Myra is still beautiful, but she progressed from being a gorgeous demure redheaded receptionist, to a legal secretary, to a paralegal, on to law school, passed the Bar exam and now is a ball-busting brunette prosecuting attorney with the local District Attorney's office. On the other hand, I have remained a completely unchanged, dedicated, poor, defense attorney representing the downtrodden (but in most cases guilty) people who have been charged with crimes by her office.

The philosophical difference between prosecution and defense attitudes can be enough to break up a marriage. This strain on the relationship is never brought out clearer than when the mind-sets collide head on at a social gathering. Most prosecuting attorneys eventually assume the zeal of people on a crusade to 'put away the bad guys,' who are all assumed to be guilty just because they've been arrested. Even the smallest file on a misdemeanor theft is no longer a case... it's a crusade, with the defense attorney looked upon as being a troublesome barrier between the D.A.'s office and justice.

The calendar clerks never put Myra and I up against each other in the courtroom, but our being on different sides of the fence has created a

Marcia Clark versus F. Lee Bailey type of atmosphere, as displayed on television every day some years back during the O.J. Simpson criminal trial. I'll never be able to figure out how that republican-democrat marriage of Mary Matalin and James Carville seems to have flourished so well unless they finally figured out how to do what my soon-to-be-ex and I never mastered: leaving all of our philosophical differences behind at the office.

Things got worse when we tried to bring our circle of friends together, because hard-nosed right-wing district attorneys with that prosecutorial badge-heavy swagger don't mix well with left-wing defenders of drug-dealers, pornographers and child molesters. But that wasn't all: when it looked like my boat restoring project was within a year of completion, we went boating with some friends and discovered that my beloved wife has a very low tolerance for motion. She can get terribly seasick at any distance more than 10 feet from the dock. Seasickness is quite common with self-centered people who have difficulty taking into consideration the boat, motion, other people around them, and a lot of other factors that contribute to the illness.

Our differences didn't stop just with the enjoyment of boating. I had to work my way through high school, college and law school by playing piano in saloons. Once we could afford a nice living-room piano, I discovered that my wife was tone-deaf and didn't like the way I played. This was definitely a marriage-counselor's nightmare, so I guess that's why while I'm out here in the back yard sitting in an old boat, my wife and her lawyer are inside that nice Brentwood home, scheming. Looking over there occasionally I notice his beady eyes peering out at my boat through the house's mini-blinds. He spends a lot of time ogling my wife and my boat... but it'll be over my dead body before he gets his hands on my boat.

I'm hoping that Stuart will tire of talking soon so I can get back to trying to fix an electrical short in the boat's wiring system before it burns the boat, and my wife's house with it. She owned the house before we were married, so she'll no doubt stay in at after I'm gone.

Fixing things on the boat are harder than I expected – mainly because I don't know what the hell I'm doing. Boat wiring is a lot different than house wiring: you can't just connect things with supermarket extension cords, because they're not heavy-duty enough to withstand the extremely harsh elements of a saltwater environment. Humans don't belong in the ocean, and the ocean keeps telling us that by trying to invade our territory just like we're invading its. An electrician friend of mine told me that I've done a nice job of cosmetically restoring this old tub, but without a complete re-wiring job it won't last too long after it's put in the water. Without a steady source of income, I'll have to cross that bridge when I come to it.

...by Reason of Sanity
Peter Sharp Legal Mystery #2

Chapter 1

There's nothing worse than a reformed smoker. I know, because I'm one. I can smell something being smoked from a car pulling up next to me in traffic with its windows open. I can smell it from someone walking upwind of me a half block away. I'm insulted by the fact that some schmuck is polluting my air.

So here I am at thirty thousand feet above the Pacific Ocean, flying back from Maui, and the fat guy sitting next to me must have smoked two packs before boarding time. It's a good thing there's no smoke detector above us because his entire huge body and clothing reek of smoke. Every time he coughs, some smoke comes out of his liver-lipped mouth. He's been sleeping for the past two hours... probably tired from all that suction.

Sitting next to this guy reminds me of a long time ago, when I was going to Chicago's Roosevelt University during the days, and working nights playing piano downtown on Rush Street. After working from nine in the evening to three in the morning in a smoke-filled saloon, I would return to my parents' second floor north Kedzie Ave. apartment, where following my mother's orders, I'd get undressed in the hallway and leave my smoke-drenched suit hanging on the stairway banister railing, to air out overnight.

But other than the odors getting to me on this flight back, this vacation was a success.

With all of the book-time spent under Lahaina's Banyan tree, in my hotel room at the Pioneer Inn and on the flights both ways, I've been able to catch up on my reading with one by Robert K. Tannenbaum, one by John Lescroart, two by William Bernhardt and then John Grisham's *The Summons,* which I think he probably phoned in. Reading books by these burnt out lawyers gives me an idea: if reformed hackers can get hired by the government as computer specialists and reformed burglars can get jobs as security experts, why can't a reformed personal injury lawyer become a defense attorney? I've certainly got the credentials. In the past year alone I settled a huge asbestosis case with nothing more than a faith healer's report... and there was the two million life insurance settlement I got for that doctor who was accused of murdering his wife. I also successfully defended my friend Stuart when a lady using his weight-loss formula sued him claiming it turned her into a nymphomaniac.

Following up on that possibility, our office sent out some inquiry letters to a couple of insurance companies I bagged last year to see if there're any hard feelings. Knowing those corporate types, they don't have feelings. To them, all that counts is the bottom line. If Hitler came back as a winning defense lawyer, he'd be on their payroll.

When checking in from Maui, I was told that one of the insurance company's defense firms might have an assignment for me.

As promised, Stuart picks me up at the flight arrival area and I get in his car, only to be bawled out during the entire ride to the Marina. He doesn't let up, obviously having heard I was thinking of changing sides. "How can you do this? You're not one of those insurance defense guys who wanna cheat injured people out of a fair settlement. Those guys ruin the lives of people who're really hurt."

"You mean like you were with that faith healer's diagnosis of fatal mesothelioma? And if I remember correctly, you didn't complain when I acted as defense attorney for you with that crazy broad who sued you for negligent nymphomania, as a result of taking that weight-loss snake oil you sell. That saved your ass and made you even richer so what's the beef?" I had him there.

"Listen Stu, I know how you feel, but if you stop to think about it, a fair defense lawyer can do more good than a plaintiff's lawyer."

"Yeah, sure. You gonna just give away your client's money?"

"No, I wouldn't do that, but if a person really is entitled to a fair settlement I can advise my client to pay it, instead of helping them interpret their policy provisions into some perverted reason not to pay."

The discussion comes to a temporary conclusion as we pull up to the C-4200 dock, where the forty-two foot Californian motor yacht I live on is docked. This isn't exactly my dreamboat, but it'll have to do until the fifty-foot Grand Banks I covet becomes affordable. We're on the same dock as George Clooney's mega yacht and I still have some hope of bumping into him and starting a friendship.

Nothing's changed while I was gone. Being close to dusk, the electric cart driven by Suzi, an adorable little Chinese girl that I inherited, is parked in its spot near the boats. That means that she and her huge Saint Bernard are on the boat waiting for me, hopefully with a gourmet meal – and some word about new clients.

Suzi runs my life as well as the practice, but she hardly ever talks to me. I still haven't figured out why, but in the last year, about the only time she addressed me was to bawl me out for getting arrested. I didn't mind that conversation because it was just after she bailed me out. Fortunately, my doctor client and I beat that bad rap, ergo the boat we're now living on... it used to be his.

Suzi's a star at the Chinese restaurant around the corner where her late mother used to work, and where the food comes from many evenings. It gets delivered by the 'Asian boys,' a polite group of four young men who do everything from bus the restaurant tables at night, to cleaning and varnishing the boats on our dock during the day.

I still can't believe how smooth it's been going for the past few months. The kid's really been through a lot. Her mother died in a car crash when she was only three, leaving her to live with her stepfather, my old law school chum Melvin Braunstein. When she finally got used to that situation, Melvin perished in a plane crash while vacationing in Thailand - and now she's stuck on a boat in the Marina living with me, her legal guardian. Living on a boat some day used to be my dream when I was a kid, so maybe she'll learn to appreciate the lifestyle too. I certainly hope so, because until she's eighteen or goes away to school, this is it.

In addition to her office routine, she also volunteers at the local hospital. They have a children's ward there, so Suzi brings her Saint Bernard in once a week to visit the children.

Her computer skills are top-notch, she runs our law practice, and has two one hundred eighty pound animals to boss around... the Saint Bernard and me.

A Class Action
Peter Sharp Legal Mystery #3

Chapter 1

If you search the world over, I don't think you'll find any guy who will admit to being a bad driver. That's what makes me so unique. The general consensus of my neighbors here in Marina del Rey is that I am one of the worst drivers in the world, and to be honest, I really can't argue with them.

This is partly due to the fact that I have very shallow depth perception, which means I can't judge distances very well. It's also partly because I've grown accustomed to driving my old, small Mazda 626 - but now I'm driving a big Yellow Hummer. This is a big change for me and I'm having a really tough time getting used to it. This difficulty got pointed out to me one day last month when I drove little Suzi to turn in her quarterly home-schooling exams. I'm her legal guardian since her stepfather passed away, and she gave me a hint about my driving by sitting in the Hummer's back seat, strapping herself in, and putting on an adult-sized football helmet. As an adorable Chinese girl who doesn't speak that much to me, she's been known to express her feelings in more graphic ways.

During my former marriage to the county's newly elected District Attorney, we also had a nice luxury car that was used for going out in the evening. She always drove. In some ways, I miss my old Mazda... and my ex-driver.

Due to the miraculous improvement in my income from the practice of law, I now have the real car of my dreams, but there's always some schmuck with a clipboard walking around, and one of them – one of my underground garage neighbors, complained to the Marina office about my driving skills. As a result, I now also rent the other two parking spaces on both sides of mine, so that nearby vehicles might be less likely to get banged by my yellow tank.

Having three parking spaces under the building is good and bad. It's bad because I have to pay extra for the other two spaces, but it's good because now there are fewer cars that can park between my spaces and the four reserved for George Clooney's limo. I've been told that his multi-million dollar megayacht is on the end-tie of our dock, and maybe now I'll have a better chance to bump into him and get friendly. After all, we are boat neighbors.

On the way back from turning in her test results, Suzi tells me she wants to make a stop on Pico Boulevard at a hobby shop just west of the Rancho Park Golf Course, so I park in front of the place while she goes in and purchases a two-foot-long, remote-controlled motor yacht. I've already learned not to ask questions about anything she does, because as the managing partner of her late step-father's law firm, technically, she's my boss.

Her stepfather was an old classmate of mine from law school, and after my suspension and subsequent divorce, he helped get me a slip near his houseboat for an old wooden Chris Craft that I was restoring and illegally living aboard. After he was killed in a plane crash and I was reinstated to practice again, I took his place in the law firm and then discovered that little Suzi was really the brains behind the whole operation. Not only is she a computer genius, she's also the star of a Chinese Restaurant around the corner where her late mother used to work. Most of the cops in our neighborhood eat lunch there every day and they've adopted her as their mascot, so we have no problem getting police reports and other little favors that most other law firms would kill for.

While Suzi practices driving her new mini motor yacht, the UPS man delivers a package for her. She must have ordered some instructional videos to help her master the art of boat handling because the package is from BOATINGDVDs.COM. It isn't until several days later while talking to some of our dock neighbors that I learn what motivated Suzi to start her maritime education efforts. Our anchorage is getting concerned with legal liability for damages caused by inexperienced people driving their boats. Unlike automobiles, there's no age or experience required to drive a boat... and these big floating trucks don't have brakes.

It's hard to stop that industrial executive from getting behind the wheel of his yacht on Sunday and taking it for a spin, even though he hasn't had more than two hours of instruction given to him by the guy who sold him the boat, and told him "it's easier than driving a car."

People don't realize that a fifty-foot boat like ours, weighing almost forty tons, has a lot of force behind it, even at only two or three miles per hour. When it bumps into another half-million dollar boat, the damages cost a lot more to repair than Emilio charges at the local body shop. You can't just slap on some bondo and send one of these yachts to Earl Scheib for a paint job.

The new Marina rules require each boat to have a valid policy of liability insurance in place, and the owner must take the Coast Guard Auxiliary's boating safety course and pass their test. In addition to these requirements, our anchorage demands that the dockmaster watch every boat's owner pull in and out of the slip, to judge their boat handling abilities.

I guess that because my non-existent boat-driving ability has caused a vacuum of respect, the job of satisfying the new Marina boat owners' requirements has been taken over by the kid. I don't want to be around to see her try to get this huge boat in and out of the slip. I know that I certainly can't do it. I think I'll concentrate on developing my driving skills on land before trying to drive our fifty-foot Grand Banks trawler yacht. In contrast, my driving experience doesn't look too bad when compared with what happened to a soccer mom today.

Tonight's local news has a story about a big GMC Suburban that blew up. Fortunately there were no serious injuries. The owner picked it up at the dealership after some routine service was performed, and drove it all around town, until there was a loud 'bang,' the engine died, and the hood flew off. No foul play is suspected, but there's surely going to be some lawyer getting involved in this... it's too strange an event to be ignored by our bottom-feeding legal community – the shysters at law.

My evening television news viewing is interrupted by a call from Vinnie Norman, a former client and present associate of my good friend Stuart Schwarzman, who is the most entrepreneurial guy I know. After getting rich off of the publicity he got from being sued for 'negligent nymphomania' when a user of a weight loss product he sells claimed to have been turned into a nymphomaniac, he went on to start several other businesses. His most profitable is the one that accepts assignments of small court claims from people who have received unsolicited 'junk' faxes. Stuart uses a recently enacted Federal Law call the TCPA, to sue those senders for five hundred dollars on each claim, and splits the recoveries with his client.

Stuart also bought an old Brinks armored truck and changed the outer signage to read: 'HE'S TAKING IT WITH HIM.' He rents the truck and a driver out to disgruntled heirs for three hundred fifty dollars: they pay to have the truck drive behind the hearse that takes their tightwad deceased to the cemetery. Vinnie drives one of the trucks for Stuart and Vinnie's fiancée Olive will be driving the second one soon.

Stuart paid for both Olive and Vinnie to get firearm training so that they could be issued Exposed Firearm Permits by the Department of Consumer Affairs. Now they can wear holstered but unloaded weapons with their uniforms when they drive the phony armored trucks in funeral processions. Everyone in this town is in showbiz.

Vinnie's current problem is causing quite a crisis in his house. After Stuart spent all that money getting Vinnie and Olive outfitted and armed, and then buying another armored truck for Olive to operate, she confessed to

Vinnie that she has a slight problem when it comes to operating the truck. She never learned how to drive.

It would have been a lot nicer if Vinnie could have had that information before, because now he fears that when Stuart finds out, his own job might be in jeopardy.

After listening to his desperate babbling for about fifteen minutes, I learn that Stuart's second armored truck won't be ready for another month or so. This means that Olive may have time to take some driving lessons and get licensed in time for her first funeral job. I don't think there's any way in hell that she'll pull it off. I know that I couldn't learn to drive that armored truck in only a month or so, and I've been driving poorly for over twenty-five years.

I wish him luck, get off the phone and start to prepare the evening meal. The special tonight will be my 'pasta ala Marina.' The only thing I know how to do is boil water and cook pasta, so my recipe repertoire consists of numerous large elbow macaroni dishes.

One fan of my cooking is Bernie, Suzi's huge Saint Bernard, who also lives with us on the boat. Whenever he sees me start to prepare some food he's at my feet the entire time, hoping for some droppings. This evening I'll be making my version of a healthy Alfredo sauce, using Land-O-Lakes non-fat half and half, Kraft non-fat grated Parmesan cheese, Smart Beat trans-fat-free butter, and some Knudsen fat-free sour cream.. As the secret ingredient, I'll be adding a new salt-free garlic salt. The result may be non-taste sauce, but at least it'll be healthy.

All of these allegedly healthy ingredients have been mandated by Suzi, who now peeks out from her domain – the foreward stateroom, when she smells the aromas. I can usually tell by her expression whether or not I'm on the right track with my formula.

Most of the time a gourmet Chinese meal gets delivered to the boat by the Asian boys, a group of young Chinese teenagers who do everything from wait on and bus tables at the local Szechwan restaurant, to varnish and maintain boats on our dock. Like most of the other people in this Marina, they adore Suzi, so one way or another I manage to have a tasty dinner.

We usually have special nights designated during each week; one for my pasta special, one for entertaining guests, one for eating out, and the others for having the Asian boys serve us dinner. Tonight it's pasta. The word must have gotten out about my new recipe, because Stuart calls to tell me he's on the way over. Suzi must have invited him after approving the bouquet wafting toward her stateroom.

I'm sure that Stuart made the initial call and wormed the invitation out of her. Now that he's signed up with some correspondence mail-order law school, he's her prize student. If not for the fact that you have to be twenty-one years old to practice law in California, she wouldn't need me at all. She runs the law practice, prepares the pleadings, does all the legal research, and pays me quite well to do her bidding in court. The other reason she can't practice law now is because she isn't tall enough to see over the counsel tables in the courtroom. When taking over as her legal guardian, I was concerned that she wasn't attending one of the local public schools. I now know that several years ago Melvin received permission for her to be home-schooled. All she has to do is go downtown every month or so to pass the Board of Education's home-schooling exams. The strange thing now is that instead of teachers coming to visit her, all I see are people coming to learn from her.

When Stuart gets to the boat he's bubbling over with his new business idea - a used car lot. I tell him that if he's looking for respect, he's going in the wrong direction. It's bad enough that he wants to be a lawyer, because there are very few jobs that rank lower in the public's scale of esteem, but used car salesman is one of them.

He explains to me that the chance to make a great profit here is too good to pass up. He owns his own warehouse in the San Fernando Valley, where he has his weight-reduction products stored and his armored trucks garaged. There's also a large enough parking lot for him to qualify for a used car sales permit, so he's going for it.

I point out to him that he's not in an area where any other car lots are, and ask him where he's going to get the cars to sell and the customers to buy them. As usual, his answer is quite remarkable.

"Peter my dear friend, you have hit the nail right on the head. Getting customers is no problem if you offer the right product at the right price – and I can do it. I've made an arrangement with I.R.S..."

"Stuart, you're not working with the government on this deal are you?"

"No, no, no. This I.R.S. stands for a New Jersey company named Insurance Recovery Sales. There's a lot of auto theft in New York, and if an insured car isn't recovered within a thirty-day period, the insurance company must pay the policy holder. If the car is subsequently recovered, the insurance company dumps it as soon as possible to these I.R.S. guys, and I can buy the cars for a little over half of the wholesale blue book."

"I don't know, Stu, you know what they say about a deal that's too good to be true..."

"Yeah Pete, I know, but I've been to New Jersey and saw their warehouse, and believe me, this deal is true."

There's no talking him out of it, so I do what I usually do every time he comes up with one of his new business ideas – wish him the best of luck and let him know that I'll be available if he needs any help.

Not too long ago, I settled his uncle's wrongful death suit. He and Suzi's stepfather both died when their plane crashed during take-off from some local airport in Thailand, where they were vacationing. That's why both Stuart and the kid are the richest people I know - until I bump into my neighbor, George.

With no important cases going on, it's time for a little relaxation, so I'm going to walk over to the Marina del Rey Junior Liquor Store to pick up a six-pack, a box of our neighbor's favorite wine, and a Playboy. On the way there, I'll stop by Laverne's boat.

The Marina has several boxy houseboats they rent out and Laverne lives in one that's on our dock. At one time she probably was a real looker, but all the looking she does now is out of the window of her houseboat, waiting for me to walk by so she can clink two wine glasses together and wink at me. I call it the 'wink and clink,' but clink probably isn't the proper word, because the glasses are plastic. They just sort of clunk.

On several occasions I've allowed myself to be led astray and spent the night aboard with her. Aside from the 'early whorehouse' décor, it's a comfortable place, and she never fails to leave some greasy French toast out for me the next morning when she goes to work.

I still don't know what she does for a living, but some husky guy picks her up every morning at seven and brings her back at six each evening. She may have a couple of years on my forty-three, but she keeps herself well-preserved in alcohol, so the deterioration's been minimal.

My plan is to stop by her boat, tell her I'm going to the market, and ask her if there's anything she needs. It's starting to get dark. I politely knock on her boat. She pops her head out of the window and after my announcement, requests some crackers and a bag of ice.

Knowing I'm in for some greasy French toast tomorrow morning, I rush to the liquor store and back. As expected, upon my return, the wink and clink are my signal to 'come aboard.' We finish off that box of wine and spend prime time watching one of those stupid reality shows that she likes. She's been known to tape an episode when not around to watch it live, making for an extremely elegant video library. The only books she has on board are some romance novels, each one showing a Fabian wannabee on the cover, shirt torn half off, and a desperate nymphet hanging on him. Every time I go to the neighborhood Ralph's Market I see those soap-opera paperbacks. I used to wonder what type of desperate person would spend their money on them.

Being only partially embalmed I can still see that the late news is showing an angry man threatening to bring a lawsuit against the dealership where his wife's Suburban was serviced. I assume that's the one that exploded.

After the wine and the news we retreat to the aft stateroom part of her floating trailer and fumble ourselves asleep.

It must be about two in the morning and I'm suddenly awake, sensing someone heavy creeping onto her houseboat. Whoever it is stops near the bedroom. I quietly sneak over to the window to get a look outside, and when I stick my head out the window, I hear a low whine. It's Suzi's huge Saint Bernard. When he sees me, he stands up against the side of the boat and I notice that my cell phone is hanging around his neck. I remove it and the dog goes back to our boat. The cell phone is turned on. After holding it for a minute or so, trying to figure out what the hell is going on, it rings.

It's FBI Special Agent Bob Snell, head of the West Los Angeles office. Not too long ago, I was instrumental in getting some information together on a gang of bank robbers, and Snell made the arrests - and took the credit. The reward money was a big contribution to the purchase of our present fifty-foot Grand Banks, so I guess you could say we've got a decent working relationship.

"Hello Sharp, are you there? It's Bob Snell... special agent Bob Snell, FBI."

"Yeah Snell, I'm here. What's the matter, you guys working overtime tonight? It's kinda late."

"I know it's late Sharp, but the reason I'm calling now is because I'd like to ask you a favor."

"I'm listening."

"Well this is kind of embarrassing, but one of our people has been arrested. We were at a party tonight honoring the retirement of a Federal Agent we all respect. After we left, one of our associates got arrested for drunk driving. She's being held in the Van Nuys LAPD Jail."

"That's a sad story, but I still don't know why you're calling me at two in the morning."

"We'd like to get her out of jail."

"So, why call me? Call a bail bondsman. They can get her out in no time. Got a pencil? Call Fradkin Bail Bonds. Their number is four seven eight,...'

He cuts me off mid-sentence. "No, no, no. We can't use a bail bondsman."

"Why not?"

"Because we're FBI agents. If the press ever found out we used a bondsman to bail out a member of the Federal Anti-Crime Task Force, they'd have a field day with it."

"So? What do you want me to do?"

"Her bail is twenty-five hundred dollars and we don't have that much cash – and they won't accept a check. We have about five hundred between us. If you can lend us two thousand, I'll give you my personal check for it, right on the spot. And don't worry, the check is good."

"Boy, what a deal. You'll take my hard-skimmed two grand and turn it into a check that I'll have to deposit and report on my income tax. What're you trying to do, make an honest person out of me?"

"Sorry Sharp, but I'm afraid that ship's already sailed. Look, can you help us out or not?"

I know for a fact that most first time offenders don't have to post bail because they get released on their own recognizance, just like a traffic

121

ticket that the cop asks you to sign. He doesn't want your autograph. He wants you to sign a promise to appear in court. What you are receiving at that time is what they call a field 'R.O.R.,' an acronym for Release on your Own Recognizance.

If I call up and talk to the Van Nuys watch commander and let him know that he's got a fed in his house, I'm sure I can get her an R.O.R.

"Okay Snell, tell you what. You and your partner meet me at the Van Nuys Jail in forty-five minutes. And when we get there, just walk with me and don't say anything. When we get to the officer at the front desk, just flip your ID's at him and have a seat in the lobby. Got it?"

"Okay, you're in charge. We'll see you there."

I call Van Nuys and explain what's going on to the watch commander. Fortunately he remembers my name, because last year I helped his boss out on a case. He tells me that the girl in custody is still pretty much out of it and he doesn't want to see her driving so soon. I assure him that she's going to be picked up by two FBI agents who will be identifying themselves at the front desk. He agrees to have her ready to go by the time we get there.

Forty-five minutes later I meet Snell and another fed outside the jail. It looks like a drug deal going down.

"Thanks for coming, Sharp. Did you bring the cash? I've got my checkbook right here."

"Don't be so hasty. You're in my ballpark now, so let's go upstairs and see if I can work some magic."

"What do you mean?"

"No questions. Just follow me and get ready to flip those fancy ID wallets when we walk in the front door."

They take my instructions and follow me up the stairs to the jail floor. As we enter the front door, there's a uniformed officer seated at a small table. I show him my State Bar card and nod to the Feds. They each flash their ID and as we walk into the waiting area, their eyes bulge out.

Only one person is sitting in the lobby. It's a disheveled female, probably in her early thirties. I ask Snell. "Is that her?"

He's totally amazed. There she is, sitting on a chair in the waiting lobby. No handcuffs, no guards, no security. "Yeah, that's her, that's Shirley."

I motion for her to come with us, and she walks over to meet Snell and his partner. She looks at me. "Am I free to go now?"

"Yes, you are. You can go with Agent Snell and his friend but you can't drive. They'll take you home and you can pick up your car tomorrow."

We all walk out together. "Sharp, I don't know how you did it, but we all thank you. Will she be going to court soon?"

I take a look at her R.O.R. papers and tell them when and where her court appearance is. She asks me for help on her case. Snell calls me aside.

"What's the deal with these drunk driving charges? Is there going to be a big fine?"

"Of course there is. Listen, my miracle working is limited. I can get someone out of jail occasionally, but there's no way I can make this drunk driving charge go away."

"Will she have to appear in court?"

"Someone's got to be there on her behalf. With the proper document signed, waiving her appearance right, an attorney can appear for her and enter a plea."

"Will you do it?"

"Yeah, I can represent her, but can she afford to pay a fee? You know, by the time the case is over the fine and court costs can add up to over a thousand dollars... but I can get her some time to pay that off."

"We can't have that."

"Whatta ya mean you can't have that? Who the hell do you think you are, The Federal Government?"

"No, no. What I mean is that if she gets a fine of anything more than twenty-five dollars, she'll lose her security clearance and get fired from her job. Can't you do something? How much is your fee?"

"Well, maybe something can be done. I charge a thousand to handle cases like this. I can see by the stunned expression on your face that you think it's a lot, so just make a check out to me for five hundred, and I'll represent her in court. The watch commander led me to believe that her Breathalyzer reading was way over the legal limit, so there'll probably be no reduction of the charge to reckless driving... but I'll talk to the judge."

Snell writes out a check to me for the five hundred dollars and makes sure to tell me that I should report it on my income tax. They all leave in his car and I go back to the Marina. Damn. Laverne is probably out like the lights on her boat, so now I won't get to earn my plate of greasy French toast for breakfast.

Conspiracy of Innocence
Peter Sharp Legal Mystery #4

Chapter 1

I'm an Internet shopper, so naturally I couldn't resist ordering a matching yellow *Hummer Shake Flashlight* from the Sharper Image. I also buy my shirts, underwear, socks, and accessories online. The only things I won't purchase online or through a catalog without first trying them on are shoes, because I firmly believe that they are one of the two things that any guy must try out for size and comfort first before making a commitment.

Stuart disagrees. He's both a good friend and a client, and last week he went to Thailand to spend some time with his new fiancée. They met as a result of her appearing in a mail-order bride catalog on the Internet. I tried to explain my shoe philosophy to him, but it was too late. He's in love, which means his brain has now been replaced with another part of his body, as the thought control center.

Getting a bride through an internet catalog is a very difficult concept for me to understand, so I Google 'mail order bride' and to my surprise, there are almost two results listed. Included are lovely ladies from the Ukraine, Russia, Thailand, China, the Philippines, the UK, Colombia, Korea, Ethiopia, and from countries that the UN probably hasn't even heard of yet. They're all looking to make an American a very happy husband, and if you order now, they'll probably throw in their country's disease du jour at no extra cost.

The phone is ringing, but the caller ID is having a problem; it can't seem to fit the caller's number in the display, so it starts blinking, in distress. I answer anyway, and to my surprise, it's Stuart. "Stu, welcome home, how was the trip. Hey, I hear there's a club in downtown Bangkok that's named 'Lewinsky's,' and their big neon sign outside depicts a moving…" he cuts me off mid-sentence with a note of urgency.

"Pete, I'm not back in the states, I'm still in Thailand, and I've got a problem that needs taking care of." I can tell by the tone of his voice that he's worried. I just hope he's not in jail, because I don't know if they have bail bond places over there. As urgent as the problem sounds though, he doesn't seem in a panic mode like most people in jail do, so I guess it must be just a business problem. He continues, and I find out that my suspicions are correct.

"Peter, I want you to do me a favor."

"If I can, Stu. What do you need?"

"I need for you to be in La Verne during the next hour. Can you do it?"

This is the most amazing request I've ever had. Stuart is one of my closest friends, and he's calling me from Thailand, to ask me to have sex with my neighbor, a lady named Laverne who lives on her houseboat, a few slips down the dock from my boat. This must be a bad phone connection, because I can't believe he's asking me that.

"Excuse me? Did I hear you correctly Stu? You want me to be in Laverne in the next hour?

"That's right, Peter, and I'm willing to pay you well for this service. Is there a problem with that?"

"I would say so, Stuart. First of all, Laverne is not home at this time of day. And second, my personal love life is none of your business, and certainly not the type of thing you should try to meddle in and insult me by offering money. What have you turned into, some sort of phone sex guy? You better get out of Thailand while you can, because I think you've crossed the line, so I'm going to do you a favor and forget you even asked me that question. Maybe it's the water that you're drinking over there, but you're certainly not acting like the gentleman I always thought you were."

"Peter, wait a minute. Oh, I see what... oh no, I didn't mean Laverne your neighbor. Heck no, I meant the City of La Verne. It's a town off the San Bernardino Freeway, next to Pomona, by the California Fairplex. I've got a customer of mine there, and the police are holding him for grand theft auto. He bought one of my used Camry's and I guess there was a glitch in the paperwork. If I don't get someone out there in the next hour with the original documentation, they're going to book my customer for grand theft auto, and I'll get sued for everything I'm worth."

Boy, is my face red. Who knew there was town out there named La Verne? I apologize to Stuart for misunderstanding him, and tell him that I'll do what I can for his customer.

I knew this would happen. Not too long ago Stuart made what he considered to be a fantastic connection with a Tony Soprano-type of character in New 'Joisy' named Billy 'Z,' who offered to sell Stuart some like-new Toyota Camrys for much less than wholesale Blue Book. After doing some investigation, we found out that they were all either stolen cars that had been recovered by the insurance company, or 'lemons' that were re-purchased by the factory. For the first several months everything was going fine, but I knew it would only be a matter of time before someone's paperwork mistake back there might catch up with one of Stuart's customers out here, and it looks like it finally did.

"Calm down, Stu, if the paperwork you've got in the office is all in order, then we should have no problem. All you have to do is send Vinnie over to the police station with the file and everything will be okay."

"I asked him, but you know Vinnie. He's deathly afraid of police stations, it's like a phobia of some sort."

I'm quite familiar with Vinnie's fear. It was especially exacerbated not too long ago when his fiancée Olive crashed into a police car while Vinnie was giving her a driving lesson.

"Okay, then what about Olive? She's not afraid of cops. Olive's not afraid of anything."

"Yeah, I know she's fearless, but I'm afraid she'd never find the police station. It's out in La Verne, on the way to Palm Springs off the 10 Freeway. Peter, you've gotta help me out on this one."

If there's anything I don't feel like doing, it's getting on the freeway before Noon. Besides, I'm supposed to attend the monthly luncheon meeting of the Venice Criminal Courts Bar Association, and if I get there on time, I can sit at the same table as my ex-wife Myra, who's the recently elected District Attorney of our county. If that doesn't work out, maybe I'll bump into Deputy City Attorney Patty Seymour. We seemed to hit it off not too long ago, and if it wasn't for the fact that Myra told me Patty was a lesbian, we might have gotten something going. She invited me to be her guest at a luncheon her club holds each month. While there, I didn't think much about the 'L.L.B.' banner hanging on the speaker's lectern, because that's the abbreviation for the degree that most of us got when graduating law school. Later that day, Myra took pleasure in letting me know that it really stands for 'Lesbian Legal Branch.'

Myra and I still disagree about Patty. Just because she attends those luncheons doesn't necessarily mean that she's a lesbian. After all, I was there too wasn't I? And I'm certainly not a lesbian. Although I must admit that I share a common interest with them because I'm also strongly attracted to good-looking women. Somewhere in the back of my mind I keep thinking that given the opportunity, I can get Patty to switch over to our side. Stuart suddenly brings me back to reality. He's still on the other end of the line, calling from an extremely long distance.

"C'mon, Pete, whatta say? I'll pay you your regular rate of a hundred fifty an hour to take care of it."

He finally gets my attention. This problem should be a no-brainer. I shouldn't have to drive to La Verne, because if I get the paperwork in time, all I have to do is hand it to Myra at the luncheon and ask her to use her cell phone to call the D.A. in La Verne and have the guy released. The whole thing should take less than five minutes, and the extra one-fifty will cover my picking up the lunch tab for everyone at our table. I can act like Diamond Jim, and Stuart will pay for it all.

"Okay, Stu, send Vinnie over here as quick as you can. The meter will start running right now, because I'm going to be forced to just sit and wait for him to get here."

Stuart agrees. Ordinarily, I wouldn't be that aggressive with my fee when it comes to helping out a friend, but taking into consideration that in the last year I was responsible for collecting around two million for him in settle-ments for his faith healer's diagnosis of the non- mesothelioma, being sued by a weight-loss client for negligent nymphomania, and for the death of his uncle in a plane crash in Thailand, I know that he's one of the richest people on the block, so there's no guilt on my part.

Vinnie will probably be here in twenty minutes, so I've still got time to call Myra and get this mess taken care of. Maybe she'll even take my word for it and have the guy released from the La Verne Police Department. I call Myra on her private line. My direct access has nothing to do with the fact that we were once married; it was a political debt she repaid for my helping to get her opponent to withdraw from the election. Unfortunately, knowing her private line number only gives me the access. Most of the time she's impossible to budge and I don't know what a favor from her office looks like.

She hasn't left for lunch yet. "Hello, this is District Attorney Scot speaking."

"Hey, it's me. Are you going to the luncheon?"

129

"Yes, Peter, I'm just on my way out of the door. What can I do for you? Please make it snappy, my driver is waiting downstairs in the garage."

"I've got some paperwork to give you, but I'd like you to take my word for it and call La Verne to have someone released."

"What's this about Peter?"

"One of Stuart's interstate car customers. The paperwork wasn't processed in time and he was picked up for GTA. I've got the original paperwork here, and if you make the call and have the guy released, I'll bring the paperwork to the luncheon and lunch will be on me for you and everyone at our table today."

"Sorry, sunshine, I can't second guess one of my deputies. One of my dividend checks came in today, so I can handle my own ten-dollar lunch. Have a nice trip."

So much for access. I'd better make a call to La Verne and make sure they know I'm on the way. Myra's Deputy District Attorney out there was in and said she'll be waiting for me at the police station. No doubt she's curious about what kind of guy could actually have bedded her boss. I've never been to La Verne before, but thanks to the wonders of Mapquest.com, I know that it's 50.27 miles from the Marina and should take me fifty-four minutes of freeway driving. I press 'Ctrl-P' for a copy of that Internet page so our office manager can include it with Stuart's invoice.

There's a knock on the hull, probably Vinnie with the paperwork. I'm glad he's finally got himself a steady job working for Stuart. When I first represented him he was directing porno movies, but now he's driving an armored vehicle for Stuart. It's one of two old converted Brinks trucks that Stuart had re-painted to read *He's taking it with him.* Stuart rents the trucks out for funeral processions and gets hired by disgruntled heirs for three hundred fifty a day. Vinnie and his fiancée Olive both now drive the armored vans for Stuart when they're not helping him out at his

130

warehouse, which is full of Camrys and weight control stuff that he sells. Vinnie comes up the boarding ladder onto the fifty-foot Grand Banks trawler yacht that I live on here in the Marina.

"Hi, Mister Sharp. I've got that paperwork for you. You know that Olive and I are getting married soon, don't you? I mean, you think it's too soon for us?"

"Vinnie, in all the years I've been giving legal advice to people, I've always refrained from telling anyone my opinion about whether or not they should get married or get divorced. That's a personal decision that you have to make on your own, and when I hear someone asking me my opinion or advice on whether or not they should take that step, it always seems like it's not me that they're asking. They're really asking themselves, and just letting me listen in on the question.

"So here's my advice. First of all, would you like to see her right now? I mean, do you spend a lot of time thinking about her and wish you could be with her? If the answer to that is yes, then you must ask yourself what you really want to do about it. If the answer is 'get married,' then don't listen to what anyone tells you. Just do it. But if the answer is that you don't think you're ready yet, then don't hurt her feelings by stringing her along and try to let her down as tactfully as possible."

'Cold feet' is an ailment that affects most men. I had it once, and now Vinnie does. Every guy in the world probably has it at least once in his life. There's no cure for it. Not even time can heal this sickness.

The drive to La Verne is completely uneventful and lacking scenery. From the 405 Freeway down the 10 and all the way past Covina, the only thing to see is traffic and industrial parks. At one point you can see Forest Lawn Cemetery, but I wouldn't exactly put that place on the tourist map. I must have made this trip hundreds of times over the past twenty years while going to Palm Springs or Las Vegas, but I've never stopped in La Verne. A friend of mine's father-in-law teaches history at the nearby university, so being a college town, I'm sure there are plenty of educated people there. Looking at some of the townspeople, I guess that La Verne hasn't passed the same ordinance we have in Marina del Rey, making it a crime for any woman weighing more than two hundred pounds to wear shorts in public.

I pull into the center of town and circle around a few times looking for a parking space. Driving a Hummer has both advantages and disadvantages, and finding a parking space to fit in is definitely one of the downsides. The Police Department offers a few 'guest' spots, but I'd have to park on top of a squad car's fender to get into the only space available, and that wouldn't be a good move in a town where you're trying to make a nice impression.

Another couple of times around the block convinces me that the only place I can conveniently get in and out of without causing any collateral damage to other cars is a passenger loading zone. The green curb is a nice contrast to my yellow Hummer, so I rationalize that the space was designed for me to park in it. Lettering on the curb states that there's a twenty-minute parking limit, but that should be no problem. I figure it'll take me less than ten minutes to completely convince them to release Stuart's customer, so I can get back here with plenty of time to spare.

I get directed to the Chief's office, where I have the pleasure of meeting with Wendy, the Deputy District Attorney, and Stan Olshansky, La Verne's Chief of Police.

As I enter the office, I notice that they're both glancing down at their wristwatches. This is not a good sign. It could mean that they're both in a hurry to get somewhere else, or that they're pissed that they had to wait so long for me to get there. After the introductions are made and the paperwork is shown to be satisfactory, the Chief picks up the phone, and acting upon an affirmative nod from Wendy, orders the jailer to cut Stuart's customer loose – with an apology.

That takes care of Stuart, but I can tell by the expressions on their faces that they're still not happy. "Hey, I've got an idea. It's almost two in the afternoon, and from the lean and hungry looks on your faces, I'd say that you haven't eaten lunch yet, so since I'm on an unlimited expense account this afternoon I'd be honored if the two of you would be my guests for lunch at the best place in town."

This suggestion definitely gets their attention. They look at their wristwatches again and both agree that the public government owes them some time to eat, so it's a done deal. Now all I have to do is get my Hummer out of that loading zone.

"Great, I'll go get my car, and we can go to lunch in style. I'll be right back." The Chief stops me.

"Oh no, Mister Sharp, that won't be necessary. One of the best places in town is a little Italian café just a block or so down Third Street. We can go out the parking lot exit of the station and walk over there in just a few minutes. They've always got my regular table reserved, so we can sit right down when we get there."

So much for obeying the law. This puts me in an awkward situation. In order to get out of that loading zone to avoid a ticket, I'll have to use the offense as an excuse to get my car. The ethics computer in my head quickly balances both the good and bad results of an admission like that and the Fifth Amendment wins. I decide not to incriminate myself and we go to lunch. Actually, I shouldn't have to worry about it, because I know the kid will add the amount of that parking onto Stuart's invoice.

Per the Chief's suggestion, we go out the back door and walk about two blocks to the Italian Café in the center of town. Sure enough, there's an outdoor table reserved for us under the canopy, and we sit down to start our lunch with some hot Italian onion buns that get immediately dipped into a small container of garlic and oil.

133

This lunch is much more enjoyable than I thought it would be. The Chief is in his thirtieth year of service and will be retiring next year. He's got plenty of stories to tell, most of them about his experiences on the job in some much larger cities. Other than a car backfiring a few blocks away, it's a quiet, pleasant afternoon lunch. The quality of this place is confirmed when I'm brought the special chopped salad I designed and ordered, which includes the usual greens and tomato plus extra chopped onions, garbanzo beans, anchovies, chopped garlic and mushrooms. As a courtesy to anyone within a ten-foot radius, I keep an extra tin of breath mints with me whenever I order my special salad. The Chief orders one of the house specialties, an angel-hair pasta dish covered with large pieces of salmon.

Wendy, the Deputy D.A. was transferred out here a few years ago from Pasadena. She's married to a court clerk and is rather dull as far as stories about experiences go, but she's friendly. When the check comes, I pick it up and walk over to the cashier's counter. While paying the bill, the cashier looks past me.

"Hey, Chief. Did you hear the gunshots?"

The Chief looks at her with a puzzled expression. "Shots? What shots?"

"Oh, about twenty minutes ago, you know, when I brought your lasagna over, there were some gunshots over on the other end of town."

She must be talking about what we thought was a car backfiring. I sign the credit card receipt and we all start walking back to the station. The Chief is using his walky-talky, bawling out someone on the other end for not notifying him about the incident. I hear the poor employee on the other end apologizing. "Gee, Chief, you've told me a million times that you didn't want to be disturbed while you were at lunch."

The Chief is anxious to get back to his office, so we're walking at a pretty brisk pace when a California Highway Patrol squad car pulls up and cuts us off just as we're about to cross the street. We stop dead in our tracks not knowing what's going on as the two CHP officers jump out of the car with their guns drawn. One of the State troopers shouts out some orders.

"Step aside, Chief. You too, lady."

The Chief and Wendy follow their instructions. There were only three of us walking together, so with those two ordered to step aside, that leaves only me. I haven't felt like this since kindergarten, when I lost out in a game of musical chairs. Both cops are now pointing their guns directly at me.

"Peter Sharp, you're under arrest for the murder of Michael Luskin. Please turn around and lock your hands behind your neck."

At least they said please.

*****

After the first four books I got a little weary trying to introduce all the main characters differently in each book, so I started putting in an **Introduction**, to make my job a little easier. Here it is:

INTRODUCTION

If this is the first Peter Sharp Legal Mystery that you're reading, it might help you to know a little background information about the characters.

Peter Sharp's wife threw him out of their home (which she actually owned), due to a conflict of their philosophies about legal representation: Peter being a defender of those poor, unfortunate people 'wrongfully' accused of crimes, and his wife Myra a prosecutor with the District Attorney's office, who railroaded them to conviction.

Peter ultimately wound up living on a dilapidated old boat in Marina del Rey, and when his former classmate/employer Melvin Braunstein died in a plane crash, Peter inherited a failing law practice, an office manager (Melvin's twelve-year old step-daughter Suzi, a Chinese computer genius) and her huge St. Bernard. Peter was appointed legal guardian, and through a series of misfortunes that miraculously worked out, wound up living with Suzi and her dog on a beautiful 50-foot Grand Banks trawler-yacht.

When Peter isn't swilling Patrón Margaritas at one of the marina's local watering holes, he's usually involved in some losing legal case that little Suzi will inevitably solve, leaving Peter with the impression that he's really as good as he thinks he is.

Along the way in each legal adventure, Peter usually winds up butting heads with his ex-wife, who Suzi adores and is constantly scheming to get back into the Sharp household. There's also Stuart Schwartzman, Peter's old friend and frequent client, who is the most entrepreneurial person in Southern California — and Jack Bibberman, the best private investigator Peter ever met.

All of the Peter Sharp Legal Mysteries are summarized at the end of this book, and if you're curious about them, more details (plus photos) are at

http://www.PeterSharpBooks.com

Magic Lamp Press   -   Venice, California

...Until Proven Innocent
Peter Sharp Legal Mystery #5

Chapter 1

Given the choice, I prefer to ride in the rear seat of any nice full-sized four-door sedan. Most people don't think there's much of a difference between the front and rear seats, but in a police car, people riding in back usually don't have the option of getting out whenever they feel like it. Take it from me... I've been there.

This evening I'm riding in the front seat of an unmarked police cruiser that's being driven by 'Tony the cop,' a boat neighbor of ours who lives aboard his old wood 40-foot Newporter Pilothouse ketch. I don't know his last name or much about him, but from what I've heard, he's a not too bad of a guy, except for maybe one shortcoming: he likes to kill people.

Tony's a twenty year veteran of the police department and is now a detective sergeant. The local newspapers liken him to Clint Eastwood's *Dirty Harry* of motion picture infamy, which is probably why the police brass is urging him to 'put in his papers' and retire. Their decision is also driven by the fact that the City Council is tired of the wrongful death lawsuits he causes. His problems also extend into the local African-American community because according to some of its most vocal members, they would like to see him publicly lynched.

Aside from being a racist, fascist, bigoted killer, he seems like a pretty nice guy. A little on the silent side, but that works for me. I estimate his height to be at least six-four, because he's a couple of inches taller than me. In addition to the height, he's obviously been a bodybuilder for many years, because his bulging muscles look like they're ready to pop right through that cheap sport coat he always wears to cover up his shoulder holster. The combination of his height, muscles, sunglasses, moustache and serious grimace work very well for him on the street, and all add up to a menacing presence.

Ordinarily I wouldn't be associating with a person of his reputation, but today I don't have a choice because the senior managing partner in our law firm promised that I'd be his guest for a Mexican dinner while he explains some problem he's having with ex-wife about the child support he's paying her.

I always seem to be getting involved in strange cases at the request of my boss, but she helps out quite a bit. Being a computer whiz, she occasionally acts in an unofficial capacity to help the local police out with some hi-tech snooping. In return, they provide her with helpful information on some our criminal cases. From what I understand, we owe Tony a favor or two for some things he did for us on a past case, so that's why I'm now on the way to his favorite Mexican dive in Culver City, where he'll probably pour his heart out to me about the mean ex-wife. So far he hasn't said anything, but that'll probably change once we get to the restaurant.

It's seven on a Wednesday evening and the place is almost empty. There's a long bar on the left side of the room, some tables in the middle, and six booths along the right side. Tony heads for the last booth and sits down with his back to the wall, so he can see the whole place. That's a paranoid habit most cops develop. I sit down opposite him, but can still see most of the place in the mirrored wall behind Tony.

The waitress finally breaks away from the two or three bar patrons and slinks over to our table.

"Hi, Tony. I had the cook start a Mexican Pizza when I saw you pull into the parking lot. It'll be ready any time now." She places two cold bottles of beer on the table. I can tell this is a real neighborhood joint because she doesn't bring any glasses.

We pick up our respective bottles, clink them together as a macho toast, and take a refreshing swig while the waitress sets our smoking hot appetizer down on the table between us. Unlike the pizzas prepared at Shakey's, this one is a large flat plate of beans and rice heaped on top of large chips, all smothered in melted cheeses. I don't know what the cholesterol and fat count of this deadly dish is, but I think Doctor Kevorkian could successfully use it on some of his patients.

Waiting for Tony to speak to me, I break off a mouthful-sized chunk of this suicide platter. While looking toward the bar, Tony seems to be reaching down to scratch his leg. Just as I put the chunk into my mouth, he decides to finally speak. It's almost a whisper.

"When I say 'now,' I want you dive down in the booth. It might even be better if you made it all the way under the table."

This is a first. I've been out to dinner with a lot of people, but no one has ever said that to me. I then realize that he wasn't reaching down to scratch his leg. He was removing a snub-nosed revolver from an ankle holster. I can see in the mirror that there's a black man standing near the bar and cautiously looking around the room.

Suddenly it happens. The standing black man reaches under his jacket and removes not one, but two large handguns that were tucked into his belt. He points one towards the bar and the other towards our booth and shouts out.

"Nobody move. Anybody move, and they're dead!"
I'm now sitting here nervously trying to make a decision. Should I dive under the table immediately, or wait for Tony's command? Unfortunately the decision is made for me, because when the bartender notices that the robber is glancing over in our direction, he pulls out his own gun and takes a shot at the black man. At that instant, three things happen simultaneously. The robber fires back at the bartender, Tony shouts 'now' at me, fires two quick shots at the robber, and I sit here

frozen in place, watching the whole show in the mirror. After firing at the robber and hitting him, Tony jumps out of the booth, runs over to the guy lying on the ground and kicks the guns out of his reach. I don't think the dead criminal was in any condition to reach for them, but I guess that's what cops are trained to do.

When Tony returns to the booth, he seems upset.

"I thought I told you to get down in the booth. You didn't move. You just sat there."

"Well yeah, I didn't want to miss the show."

I hear some sirens in the distance, so the cavalry must be on the way. Tony must think I'm either completely crazy, or the coolest character on the planet. He calms down a bit and lets me know that I'm on my own for a ride home.

"You might as well finish the pizza... it'll be on the house. When the uniforms get here, I'll be busy for the rest of the night. That's the big problem with shootings – there's too much paperwork involved. You better plan on taking a cab back to the Marina."

When the men in blue come in through the front door, Tony stands up and displays his badge. They take his weapon and escort him outside. For some strange reason, the whole incident has made me hungry, so I'm now pigging out on the pizza while waiting for them to come and take my statement. I'm sure that the police brass and the City Council will be unhappy with tonight's event. Too bad they won't even take into consideration the fact that Tony stopped an armed robbery and probably saved the lives of several people, one of them being especially important to me.

The Common Law
Peter Sharp Legal Mystery #6

Chapter 1

Marriage can be a great institution, but I don't do too well in institutionalized situations, so mine didn't work out – and that's too bad, because my ex-wife Myra was elected as our county's District Attorney and I missed out on all of those fancy black tie events offering free food and an open bar.

We got along just fine during the first couple of years we were married, but then she decided to start law school. Why not? I guess she figured that if I could do it, anyone could. It was all downhill from there. I think that some females are born with a prosecution chromosome that prevents anyone around them from ever getting away with anything. Most women utilize that trait as mothers; others become teaching nuns or deputy district attorneys. Myra was very fortunate in having been able to achieve her maximum genetic potential... she's the chief prosecutor of Los Angeles County. My law practice requires that I do some criminal defense work, so she now gets some opportunities to do to me what I used to enjoy doing to her.

At first there was a feeling in the legal community that because the D.A. is my ex-wife I'd be getting some preferential treatment from her office. Unfortunately though, all the feelings have been proved wrong. Aside from my being wrongfully arrested a few times in the last year or so, I'd say that I've been getting treated fairly by her gang, but anyone who spends time in the downtown Criminal Courts building knows that there's no love lost between us. As a result of my helping her to get elected she gave me her private telephone number so I now have instant access to her, but that's all the thanks I ever received. So much for gratitude.

My good friend Stuart Schwarzman is the complete opposite. He hasn't got a prosecutorial bone in his body, is easygoing, and always concerned about the rights of every person. He isn't married at the present time, or at least I don't think he is, so when he calls to ask my advice about a domestic situation he claims to be involved in I remind him of my general rule to not do 'phone law' and invite him to stop by my boat later this afternoon so that we can talk about his alleged issue face-to-face.

With the help of a certain computer freak who rarely talks to me, my law practice has been doing quite well, and I was able to afford a partnership share in this 50-foot Grand Banks trawler-yacht here in Marina del Rey, California, which is where I live and run my practice. We're out on the western edge of Los Angeles, so the constant ocean breeze protects us from most of the city's smog.

I normally wouldn't have a mini-family living with me on the boat, but in Mel's last Will and testament he requested that I be appointed Suzi's legal guardian. She's an adorable little 12-year old Chinese girl with exception logic and computer skills. I never thought that the court would approve me, and I still suspect that Myra must have had something to do with the judge's decision. Like everyone else, both Myra and the judge fell in love with Suzi at first sight and couldn't resist her plea to be allowed to continue her lifestyle of living on a boat in the marina, like she did with her stepfather on his houseboat. A portion of the multimillion-dollar settlement I was able to get her from Melvin's death bought made her my partner in this boat, and allowed us both to move up: her from Mel's small old houseboat, and me from a client's old wooden cabin cruiser I was staying on. Our Grand Banks is a beautiful boat, but pales in comparison to the 138' mega-yacht everyone says is owned by George Clooney that ties up out on the end tie of our dock. One of these days I hope to bump into him, but so far all of my efforts at meeting him have failed.

After Melvin was gone I discovered that Suzi is a home-schooled genius and was always the brains behind her stepfather's small law firm and her huge beast is a great watchdog. He knows who the 'friendlies' are and Stuart is one of them, so there's no growling whenever he comes to visit the boat.

The other friendlies who can come aboard at will are Stuart's employees Vinnie and Olive, my investigator Jack Bibberman, Suzi's adopted big sister, my ex Myra, all of our dock neighbors, and just about every cop on the west side of town who make frequent visits to the boat to avail themselves of Suzi's computer skills and access to secure criminal databases – with passwords she probably 'borrowed' from Myra's computer during one of her sleep-overs at what used to be our house in Brentwood Glen.

Suzi is always trying to create some scheme to get Myra and I back together again, but we're both onto her plan, so we just play along, so as not to upset her. Unfortunately, the good ship *reconciliation* has already sailed, and I'm afraid I've missed the boat.

The loud knocking on our hull is probably Stuart. The way this 40-ton boat is starting to rock means that he's coming up the boarding ladder, and we're glad it's a strong one, because he'll never see 250 again... if he can even see the scale at all, while he's standing on it.

"What's up Stu? I haven't heard from you in a while. By the way, did that deal you were working on to sell your house last year ever come through?"

"It's funny you should ask, because that's the problem. I'm facing a big capital gains liability."

"That's what happens to successful people Stu. They buy low, sell high and pay taxes on their profits. But that's not exactly a domestic situation... it's a tax problem. "

"I think I've figured out a way around that. My accountant says that as a single guy I'm allowed to avoid paying taxes on the first quarter million of profit. But if I'm married and filing jointly with my wife, the exemption is doubled to a half mil... and I'll be going for the much bigger exemption."

"Yeah Stuart, I've heard about that law. I think you'd have had to be married and living there with your wife for two of the past five years in order for that exemption to kick in. Maybe you can find some girl to marry and backdate the marriage certificate. Don't look at me like that! I'm just kidding." It's hard to feel sorry for Stuart and his tax liability. He's got several successful businesses going on and as a result of some cases I've settled for him in the past, he's also got a couple of million dollars stashed away somewhere. Another thing he's always successful at is never failing to surprise me.

"I was married. I mean I'm still married. I mean, I have a wife, and we file joint returns."

"Stu, are you telling me you're currently married? How come I've never met her?"

"You have met her Pete."

"What are you talking about? You've never introduced any woman to me as your wife. Are you secretly married to someone?"

"Well yeah, I guess you could say that."

"Is it someone I know? What's this lucky female's name?

"Her name's Priscilla and you've met her... at least you've seen her around my office."

I'm struck silent for a minute. Of all the times I've been to Stuart's office the only woman I've seen there is Olive, and she's engaged to Vinnie - Stuart's other employee.

My thoughts are temporarily interrupted by the sound of large paws approaching. It's the beast and its master. Usually she just opens the door to her private foreward stateroom to listen in on the conversations I have, but this time it must have gotten too interesting, so they've decided to come out into the open and eavesdrop in person.

As I rack my brain trying to remember Stuart introducing me to any dame named Priscilla, Stuart saves me the trouble.

"Don't strain yourself Pete. Priscilla's not a woman. I mean, she's female, but not a woman."

"What do you mean it's not a woman? You mean you're married to some girl child named Priscilla?"

I'm dead serious, but this last question of mine forces a giggle out of the kid. It's the first time I've ever seen her do that since a funny car commercial we saw last year.

"Calm down Pete. Priscilla is my cat. You've seen her at the office a million times. She sleeps on top of my warm computer monitor during the day."

"Come on Stuart. This is getting a little too weird for me. I never expected this kind of craziness, even from you."

"I know it sound nuts Peter, but I had to do it for tax purposes. By the way, all this stuff we talk about today is privileged, isn't it?"

I can't believe what I'm hearing, but I think I know where he's going with this. The kid obviously figured it out already because behind me I hear large paws leaving the room and then the foreward stateroom door being closed. "Yes Stuart, it's privileged."

"Pete, please listen. I'm not crazy or weird. A couple of years ago when I saw how the property values in my neighborhood were starting to go through the roof, I knew that my old house would be a valuable item. I bought it over twenty years ago for only thirty-five grand, and now others not even as nice as mine down the street started selling for over four hundred big ones. Over the years I put in a nice pool, air conditioning, a big family room addition and lots of other improvements to make it the nicest place on the block.

"Several local real estate agents told me that if property values in my neighborhood kept going up like they were, I might be able to get over six hundred G's for the place, so I made some tax-saving plans.

"The government doesn't come out to verify what a person's wife looks like, so I applied for and received a social security card for Priscilla and started filing joint returns with her as my wife. My tax guy isn't a close personal friend, so he never knew. I only contact him once or twice a year, and didn't retain him until about a year after my cat marriage, so he never questioned it.

"As husband and wife we took the full half-million-dollar capital gains income tax exemption instead of one half that size. And there was no misrepresentation either, because it was our main residence for at least two of the past five years. We were just following the law."

I put my hand up as a signal for him to stop talking. I need a brief period of silence to gather my thoughts. As I rub my forehead, I find that no words are coming to mind. This new stunt of his has left me completely speechless.

"Okay Stuart, here's the way I see it. You're not really married to that cat, and there are so many reasons why, that I don't even want to start to explain them all. Suffice it to say that if you want to play out this little charade for tax purposes, my advice is to not do it.

"With your marriage plan, the State of California's refusal to recognize common law marriage probably doesn't apply because you're not using it for purposes of inheritance, insurance, property rights or any other reason where the state's law comes into play. The I.R.S. doesn't care about most individual state laws with respect to domestic relations, so maybe you can get away with it. I don't know, but I advise against it anyway."

I don't know what else to say. He's really gone over the top this time, and I don't want to dignify this ridiculous situation by responding to it with any type of discussion about the law.

"Thanks for your input Pete, but I think that as long as I've reported all my income, the worst that could happen during an audit is that they'd disallow the extra exemption and I'd have to pay the tax. As long as you report your income, they don't get too mad at you. From what my tax guy tells me, you have to fail to report at least fifteen percent of your income before a criminal investigation kicks in, and I've reported every penny of mine. Everyone cheats a little on deductions. Nobody goes to jail for it and believe me - my tax guy is an expert on that subject."

The secret of Stuart's financial success has always been an uncanny ability to find some small way to change the odds just a little bit toward his favor. The way he once explained it to me was like a game of blackjack in Las Vegas. As far as games go, Stuart thinks that blackjack is the one with the best odds of a customer winning. Those odds are still with the 'house,' but at blackjack the player has some kind of chance if he doesn't do anything stupid. The question Stuart asked me was "what if you played blackjack in Las Vegas, but were legally allowed to see what card the dealer had face down on the table?" His logic becomes apparent. Even if you could see the dealer's 'hole' card, there's no guarantee that you'll win every hand, but just that little edge gives you a slight boost in the odds, because of your knowing when the dealer will have to either hit or stand pat.

This marriage scam of his is no different. Once again he wants to skew the odds. I can see there's no sense in continuing to argue with him because his mind is obviously made up, and that's that. But who am I to question him? He's avoided being arrested so far in his life, and he's wealthy, so maybe he's right and I'm wrong.

"By the way Pete, are you doing anything special next Thursday afternoon?"

For some strange reason I don't like the sound of his question. It's too innocent. "I don't know, Stu. What do you have in mind?"

"Well, I got this letter from the I.R.S. and it seems that they'd like me to stop by their office next Thursday to clear up some questions they have about my capital gains tax marriage exemption."

The other shoe just dropped. I had a feeling he might be leading up to something like this.

"Stuart, I might be wrong about this, but I think that's what they call an audit. I don't know too much about tax law, so you'd be much better served by having your C.P.A. go there with you... and bring your checkbook, because they might not look favorably at your wife not exactly being human."

"You mean I might get arrested?"

"I think that commitment to an asylum would be more likely. Talk it over with your C.P.A. He'll handle it for you. I also think that if a representative appears on your behalf, there's no need for you to be there. Come to think of it, that would be a good idea. If your representative doesn't know anything about Priscilla's lower classification in the food-chain, and you're not there, there's less of a possibility of that little detail leaking out."

"That's a slight problem Pete. My tax guy can't make it next Thursday."

"If he's a C.P.A., there's probably someone else in his office that can handle the appearance for you. He is a C.P.A., isn't he?"

"Not exactly."

"That's okay. Even if he's not a C.P.A., as your accountant, he can still make the appearance on your behalf." He is a real accountant, isn't he?" I can tell by the hesitation what Stuart's answer probably is to my question. I just hope he hasn't been having his taxes done in some storefront fortune-teller's place.

"C'mon Stuart. If he's not a C.P.A. and he's not even an accountant, what the hell is he, your gardener?"

"No, no, it's nothing like that. He really knows his tax law, it's just that he's unavailable next Thursday."

"That's no problem. I'm sure you can get a continuance of your appointment until your guy is available."

This causes more hesitation on Stuart's part. It looks like he's racking his brain for another excuse he can make for his accountant.

"They might not want to continue the appointment until he's available... I mean, it might be a while."

"You mean he's that busy?"

"No. He's out of town."

"Exactly where out of town? Timbuktu?"

"3901 Klein Boulevard. That's in Lompoc, California."

For some strange reason that address sounds familiar. Whoa, it just hit me. Some time ago I had to go up to Lompoc to visit a former client, and if my memory serves me correctly, that's the location of a correctional facility. "Stuart is your accountant currently a guest of the federal government?"

Stuart looks down towards the floor. Why am I not surprised?

"Stuart, I suppose you know that address is a federal penitentiary. Is your tax accountant a convicted felon doing hard time?"

Stuart's silence says enough.

"How did you happen to find this criminal? His ad in the yellow pages?"

"No. We met in a tax chat room on the Internet. He sounded really knowledge-able, so we made a deal for him to do my income taxes, and at first I didn't know he was in prison. I knew he wasn't local because all my written correspondence to him was sent to a P.O. Box in Buelton, California. I now know that's a town near Lompoc, where some of the prisoners are allowed to receive mail.

"He did my taxes for the first two years and I was really satisfied with his work. It wasn't until I wanted to meet with him in person to discuss my capital gains problem that he confessed to me he was serving time. He let me know that he would understand if I decided to pull my business and find another accountant... one on the outside.

"I appreciated his honesty with me, went up there to visit with him a couple of times and realized that I'd have to find someone on the outside to help me with the audit.

"And that's where it stands now. I know that you're not a tax lawyer Peter, so there're no hard feelings in your not wanting to go with me next week. I'll find someone else. There're a lot of accountants in the San Fernando Valley."

I'm glad he understands my reluctance to get involved in his beastial tax matter.

Ever since Stuart started classes at some fly-by-night correspondence law school his main purpose in visiting our boat is to meet with Suzi, who is tutoring him in his studies and helping him brief some cases.

Realizing that his discussion with me has now come to a dead end, Stuart goes to the foreward stateroom, knocks and enters. As he closes the door behind him I hear the kid's voice. "Hello Stuart. How's the wife?"

The Magician's Legacy
Peter Sharp Legal Mystery #7

Chapter 1

Several years ago a network television station aired some shows that featured a masked magician who dared to reveal secrets about how the most popular magic tricks and illusions are performed. He wore the mask as protection from alleged physical threats from fellow magicians who felt betrayed. I watched part of the first show, but skipped the rest of it and its several sequels because I just don't want to know how it's done.

I love magic. Every time I watch a magician perform I turn into a little kid, with my mouth and eyes wide open. I enjoy being fooled, and the more I'm tricked, the more I like it. Knowing how it's done would spoil the fun for me and I don't want that to happen.

It looks like not everyone is like me. They're nosy. They all want to know how the magicians do it. People like that suffer from a personality disorder that prevents them from believing someone is smarter than they are. They refuse to accept the fact that they can be fooled by another mere mortal... they selfishly push to find out what the 'trick' that confused them was, so they can then regain their fragile confidence and once again believe that they are superior beings, only having been temporarily fooled by some unfair gimmick that they now know about.

And as for the people who do the tricks, whenever I encounter some guy with the adjective 'great' preceding his name, one that invariably ends in a vowel, I want to be entertained. I want to be fooled. I want to see that rabbit come out of a hat, the colored silks, the self-repairing rope and the three rings that come apart and go back together again. I love it. And of course at my age, it's even better if the magician has some long-legged female assistant in high heels that helps in the misdirection. It certainly works every time with me, but I'm a normal forty-three-year-old male lawyer. It doesn't work for Suzi, the little Chinese cupie doll I live with.

She's a computer genius and the brains behind our law firm... the one that was started by her stepfather and is now headed up by me, due to a fatal airplane accident that not only left me in charge of the law practice, but also as her legal guardian. We both live aboard a 50-foot Grand Banks trawler yacht here in Marina del Rey California, along with Suzi's huge Saint Bernard that I call Bernie, because he's got some Chinese name that I can't pronounce.

The kid doesn't have many friends her age, but she does see another little girl named Lotus Chang, whose mother Michelle is a customer at Murray's Chinese restaurant, around the corner on Washington Boulevard, where Suzi's mother Jasmine was the manager. Jasmine was having trouble with her citizenship status, so a customer at the restaurant, and old law school classmate of mine named Melvin Braunstein, helped out by marrying her. When Jasmine was killed in an automobile accident about a year later, Melvin did the legal work for his stepdaughter and succeeded in settling it for quite a bit. As a result, Suzi is the richest little girl in the Marina.

When Melvin perished in a private plane crash, his Will appointed me as Suzi's legal guardian. A year later, I succeeded in getting a huge settlement for her from the distributor of faulty counterfeit airplane parts: that enriched the kid's trust fund by another couple of million dollars. As official administrator of her bank accounts I get paid a whopping CEO salary of one dollar per year, and our little law practice seems to be thriving, so we're living on a beautiful yacht named the 'Suzi B' that I don't even know how to start the engine of. The fees keep coming in, I have my big Yellow Hummer to ride around in, and there's an alcoholic broad named Laverne living on a houseboat near us who is an altogether different kind of hummer that I ride occasionally. Life is good.

Michelle Chang invited Suzi to Lotus's surprise 11th birthday party, so I'm all alone on the boat tonight trying to get some research done, with a 200-pound Saint Bernard asleep across my feet. Unfortunately, I wasn't invited to the party, which is too bad, because I understand that Mrs.

Chang hired a professional magician from the Magic Castle to come and entertain the kids. I tried to tell her that whenever a magician is around, I'm a kid too, but it didn't work.

When the kid's here, we often have some gourmet Chinese dinners delivered from Murray's, by a group of four young fellows nicknamed the 'Asian Boys' who work evenings at the restaurant, and varnish boats during the day. With no kid and no Asian Boys, my dinner tonight will consist of the usual pot of gruel that I've perfected over the years. The recipe involves eight ounces of elbow macaroni plus the addition of one or more of several flavoring items that can vary between non-fat cottage cheese, non-fat baked beans, non-fat butter, green peas, low-fat cream of mushroom soup, non-fat vegetarian chili, or whatever else I happen to find within reaching distance.

Whatever the final mixture is, it all gets topped off with a generous sprinkling of imitation Parmesan cheese and some garlic salt, and most of it never makes it to the table because it gets eaten right near the stove. I've been told that single men are the only variety of humans that are known to eat standing up.

This time there's enough 'Pasta ala Peter' prepared to be finished up sitting down in the yacht's main saloon. Like so many other uninformed boaters, I used to call it the 'salon,' but some balding old jerk with a fifty-foot sailboat on our dock bawled me out when he heard me call it that, and demanded that I use its correct designation. I try to show respect to my know-it-all elder, so now it's the main 'saloon.'

The dog is always alert whenever I'm eating, because he's on constant 'crumb patrol,' but I don't mind him around on evenings like this because he's an excellent listener. Tonight's seminar is on the double job that's usually required whenever a lawyer takes on certain types of cases, one of them being for legal malpractice. The extra work is because not only does the new lawyer have to prove that the original lawyer was guilty of screwing up, but he must also show that if the case was handled properly that the client could have actually won. This means that not only do you have to destroy the first lawyer, but you also have to go ahead and

154

almost completely re-create the first trial, showing how it should have been won. And that's the reason I don't take cases like that.

Both the dinner and the dissertation have been completed and not one living thing in the room disagrees with me about either... another successful dinner lecture.

The birthday party must be over now because Mrs. Chang just called to let me know that she'll be bringing Suzi back to the Marina. I was supposed to pick her up, but I like to think that this favor is motivated by a combination of her wanting to give Lotus more time with Suzi - and her desire to see me. Ego self-inflation has always been one of my strong suits.

When they all arrive at the boat and dump some party stuff on table I see that once again my thoughts were wrong, because it's Mrs. Chang who's the one spending more time with Suzi. Michelle is in the IRS's Intelligence and Enforcement Division, and is fascinated by all the crime-fighting software that the kid has 'collected' on her computer, as a result of being so closely associated with my ex-wife (who is now the elected District Attorney of Los Angeles County) and all the cops who consider her a mascot. This mascot status is because of the kid's daily noon appearances at the Murray's Chinese restaurant around the corner, where her mother used to work. It's also the place where squad cars from all the local police agencies converge for lunch, or as Suzi informs me, a 'Code 7,' which in police-speak means 'out of service, to eat.'

One remarkable feature about this Chinese restaurant is an official-looking sign posted in the men's room that I've been told commands 'employees to their wash hands before returning to work.' Good idea, but in a Chinese restaurant with Chinese immigrant employees, you'd think they might have the sign in some language other than Spanish.

Word about Suzi's computer skills and searching abilities have gotten around and enabled our firm to pick up quite a few clients and gather some future favors from local law enforcement groups. Her popularity is also due to some of the missing forms from our file cabinet that were probably used to help many of those cops defend the divorce actions that police wives are wont to file.

Unlike Suzi, little Lotus Chang is quite talkative around me, so while her mother is busy with my boatmate in the foreward stateroom, I get a full narrative about how the birthday party went. Listening to this little girl rattle on and on makes me more appreciative of the fact that Suzi rarely talks to me, opting instead to make most communications by 'dog-mail,' which consists of tucking a message into the Saint Bernard's collar and sending him to me.

Most of Lotus' story is about the other kids that attended the party. Not interested. She goes on to provide me with a detailed list of every present she received at the party, complete with a full description of each and every gift-giver. Still not interested. My eyelids are now getting heavy.

Among the party debris still defacing our beautiful expensive teak table are some Polaroid photos taken at the party, and one of them I find particularly interesting because it shows a strikingly attractive woman standing next to an older man. At first I thought that they must be the mother and grandfather of one of the kids attending the party, but as Lotus drones on, she informs me that the photo in my hand is Mister Robert Balscomb, previous owner of the Changs' house.

Lotus says that Balscomb stopped by with Marian, his housekeeper. The reason for their invitation to the party was that Marian is Michelle Chang's former porcelain-painting teacher, and the person who originally told Mrs. Chang about Balscomb's house being for sale. Michelle wanted to show off how her porcelain collection is displayed, so Mister Balscomb came along to do the driving and give Mrs. Chang some pointers on features of the 'safe room' where she keeps her collection. When Balscomb owned the house he paid big bucks to convert the den into what security experts call a 'panic room,' complete with bulletproof walls and emergency communication devices. He's obviously either paranoid, or has a very checkered past he's afraid might catch up with him.

Lotus notices that I can't seem to stop looking at the picture of Balscomb and his companion, and surprises me.

"Gee, that's funny… Marian kept looking at your picture too."

"What are you talking about Lotus?

"That picture of you and Suzi. You know, the one you guys took at her birthday party last year. She gave it to me for my 'friends' collection, and when Marian, the lady in the picture with Mister Balscomb, saw it, she kept looking at it the same way you're looking at that picture of her."

This is interesting. It's almost like computer dating, because we seem to be interested in each other's pictures. Maybe I should call her. This might present a slight problem. Somewhere in the back of my mind I get the feeling that Lotus' mother Michelle might be interested in me. That's flattering, but I could never get involved with anyone connected with the IRS… but at the same time, I don't want to hurt her feelings. I'm going to see this Marian, but it will have to be a covert operation at first.

Lotus says that Suzi didn't think much of Mister Robert Balscomb. If you're not a uniformed law enforcement officer it's tough to get her respect. She's a cop groupie, so it's not surprising to hear she didn't warm up to Balscomb. What does surprise me is hearing that Balscomb was so impressed by the magician entertaining the kids that he stayed for the whole performance and seemed to enjoy it as much as the kids did. He also made sure to get one of the magician's business cards before leaving.

The Changs are leaving the boat now and my phone is ringing. It's my close friend Stuart, who rarely calls just to say hello. He's the most entrepreneurial person I know, and now has at least five successful businesses going that I'm aware of. Whenever I see his familiar telephone number on my caller I.D. display I assume it's either because he needs some emergency legal advice or wants to tell me all about some new business he's going to start up.

"Hello Stuart, what's up?"

"Peter, I'm angry."

"Okay Stu, why don't you just calm down and tell me about it."

"You're going to think it's too trivial and you'll probably laugh at me."

"Stuart, I promise I won't laugh. I've been practicing law and listening to clients for almost twenty years now, and my legal bedside manner has developed to the point where I can control any urge to laugh at what I'm being told, so go ahead, let's hear about it. Does it have anything to do with money?"

"Yes Pete, it does."

"All right, now we're getting to the heart of the matter. What's the amount?"

There's silence on the line as Stuart hesitates with his answer. This probably means that the amount he got screwed out of is so large that he's embarrassed to tell me. "C'mon Stu. You called me, so if you won't tell me the amount, then I'd like to get off the phone and go back to some things I'm doing around the boat."

"Seventy cents."

Stuart never fails to surprise me. "Stuart, I know in my heart that the amount can't be bothering you, because next to Suzi you're one of the richest people I know. There's must be something else that's bothering you about that trifling sum, so please, let me know what it is."

"You're right Pete. It's not the amount, it's the principle of the thing. I picked up a chopped salad to-go at a restaurant. It was eight dollars and fifty cents."

"So?"

"So, they charged me sales tax on it!"

"What's the big deal? You pay sales tax on everything else you buy that's not for resale, so why complain this time?"

"Peter, you went to law school. Didn't they teach you that there's not supposed to be sales tax charged on food to-go?"

"Sorry Stu, I must have been absent that day. Are you sure about the law on that matter?"

"Not exactly, but I pick up a lot of carry-out food, and to the best of my recollection, this is the first time I've ever been charged sales tax on it. I should think that while the exact percentage amount might vary between jurisdictions, the main policy decision of whether or not it's due on food-to-go is a statewide decision and should be consistent."

"So what do you intend to do about it? Turn them in to the State Board of Equalization, or Franchise Tax Board, or whatever agency handles that stuff? Or are you planning some huge class action on behalf of all the taxpayers in the State? Either way, I don't think I'm with you on this one. At least not with the facts the way they are to this point."

"Oh yeah? Well what would you do if you were me?"

"First, I'd go back to that restaurant and show them two receipts: one from another nearby restaurant that didn't charge the tax on a similar item to-go, and also the receipt from their own register on which the tax was added. I'd also make sure that I talked to someone in the restaurant who was in charge, because there's always the possibility that the sale was rung up by a new employee or someone else there who just made a common mistake and pressed a wrong classification button on the cash register.

"If you handle it like a gentleman, I'm sure you'll get a happy conclusion. If a mistake was actually made, any competent manager should probably apologize to you and might even offer you a dinner on the house for pointing it out to them. But first and most important, please go to the State's local tax office and find out what the law really is. It's obvious that one of those restaurants made a mistake, and it's either the one that charged you, or the one that didn't. I think you owe it to them as a neighbor to point out the error to the wrongdoer, and not just rush to turn them in or file a lawsuit."

Stuart grudgingly agrees with me and says he'll check out the law. After hanging up I start going through several party favors spread around on the table, hoping there's some leftover birthday cake included, and happen upon a business card that announces 'The Great Schwartzi." This is obviously the party magician's card. The surprising part is what's written on the blank back side of the card. It's a local address, with a scribbled note that says 'Suzi, I'll expect you at my house tomorrow at one P.M.'

The Reluctant Jurist
Peter Sharp Legal Mystery #8

Chapter 1

While watching an interesting television news documentary about manufacturing in China, I was surprised to learn how many fine products they make there. Unfortunately, they're almost all fakes. They make copies of the best of everything, including wristwatches, purses, golf clubs, luggage, DVD's, clothing and just about any other internationally known successful brand name products. The 'knock-offs' they produce sell for as little as one twentieth of what the genuine thing would ordinarily cost here in the U.S.

Once the counterfeit merchandise reaches this country it gets bought up by people who don't really care that it's phony, because it looks real. No one cares that the wristwatch may stop running next month, because during that month it will have served the main purpose of image boosting. Notwithstanding the fact the watch company certainly is justified in protecting its copyright, it should also realize that any person who spends forty bucks for a phony Rolex would never spend eight grand for a real one, so they shouldn't whine about losing a customer they never would have had to begin with.

The 'knock-off' mentality doesn't stop with the counterfeiting of merchandise. It extends to many types of scams against governments and organizations, like welfare fraud, exaggeration of income tax deductions, staged auto accidents, phony workmen's compensation claims, inflation of corporate income to bolster stock prices, and many more types of scams, and the new class of perpetrators are no longer just small time street hustlers. Many of them now wear tailored Italian suits and spend their time in boardrooms... but whether next to a wall on the street - or on Wall Street, they all share the common trait of a complete disregard for business ethics... and I'm sorry to say that the legal profession is not without its bad apples.

As for my own situation, I live on a genuine fifty-foot Chinese-built Grand Banks Trawler Yacht here in Marina del Rey California, along with little Suzi Braunstein, a genuine Chinese-built pre-teen girl and 'Bernie,' her huge Saint Bernard. Both the girl and dog are part of a package deal foisted upon me when her late stepfather's Will requested that I be appointed as her legal guardian. Suzi is a cupie doll with genius computer skills that are often put to use fulfilling requests from many of the local cops who eat around the corner at Murray's Chinese restaurant, where her late mother was the manager. Suzi still makes her daily lunchtime appearances there and has become sort of a 'mascot' to all of the uniformed police regulars who eat there often and where they hold their monthly inter-agency law enforcement luncheons.

The one problem I'll never have to worry about with Suzi is her asking me for an allowance – and that's because she's worth several million dollars, as the result of civil settlements from the death of her mother in an auto accident and her stepfather in a plane crash. But even without that money she would still be okay, because with her incredible computer skills she could easily earn six figures a year. But that'll never happen because she's already got a job. She runs our little law firm... the one we operate off of this boat. She's the brains and has a couple of two hundred pound animals to boss around. I'm the one that makes the court appearances.

We've been doing pretty good as of late, so I don't have any financial problems either, which can be boring. It was a lot different years ago when my ex-wife and I were newlyweds. I was a struggling lawyer and my wife Myra was a legal secretary. When we got married, the common bond that held us together was our mutual efforts to pay the rent, drive dependable cars, and have decent wardrobes. That was definitely not a boring time, and stayed that way until my practice started to pick up and she started law school. The money problems were slowly coming to an end, but the philosophical conflicts were starting to replace them. Like most women, my wife was born with a 'prosecution' chromosome in her genome. Being a good-natured criminal defense attorney, my DNA doesn't include one of those... and that's where the problems began.

What happened to our marriage is public record. It includes my disciplinary problems with the State Bar, her passing the Bar exam and getting hired as a Deputy District Attorney, our divorce, and then her inheriting a zillion dollars from her grandfather.

I was finally able to prove that my being disbarred was a frame-up, so my ticket to practice law was returned, but I still regret missing out on a chance to share in Myra's inheritance. I always seem to be surrounded by millionaires who never want to share. Once my wife decided to downsize the household, I became history and was exiled to an old forty-foot wooden cabin cruiser I had been restoring in our back yard, which thanks to my dear old classmate Melvin Braunstein, ultimately wound up here in the Marina.

While actively practicing law again I created a strategy that convinced Myra's opponent to withdraw from the election, so she is now the elected District Attorney of this county, and I'm a successful attorney, no thanks to anything she's ever done for me. If it wasn't for little Suzi's constant conspiring to get Myra and I back together again, we probably wouldn't even be speaking too much - but today is one of the days we will be, because Suzi needs a ride downtown to take another one of her periodic home-schooling progress tests.

Her grades in the past were so high that the Board of Education's big shots now insist she take her exams under their proctoring so they can make sure she's not cheating. Those bureaucrats just can't seem to believe that this kid is smarter than they are. Suzi doesn't complain about the in-person testing requirement because it gives her a chance to see Myra, who has become a role model for her. She also doesn't mind taking the tests in person, because it eliminates the need for a home-school teacher to certify the test results. I have a sneaking suspicion that there is no home-school teacher, because I've never seen one around. I think the kid teaches herself by using a class teaching schedule, a lesson plan, the internet, and a local library.

Whatever she's doing seems to be working, because her test scores are usually almost perfect, which doesn't stop her from talking Myra into joining us on these test days, under the guise of needing some extra moral support. We all know that's not true, but it does bring us I together for lunch.

Myra and Suzi sit holding hands in the back seat of my big Yellow Hummer and Bernie has a permanent claim on the front passenger seat, so he can ride with his head poking up out of the open sunroof. Suzi bought him a pair of 'Doggles' to wear. They're aviation-style eye-protection goggles designed for dogs to wear while riding in cars with their heads sticking out in the wind. With his Doggles on and those big ears flapping in the wind, he looks like a World War I air ace. We've dubbed him the Brown Baron.

We're quite an impressive sight driving down the Los Angeles streets, with the Baron's head sticking out of it's cockpit and camera-toting tourists photographing us. Without a picture to prove it, they'd never be able to convince their friends back home about the unique sight they saw here of the big Swiss-made Saint Bernard wearing his Doggles.
Not too long ago we heard that some mainland Chinese menus include Saint Bernard meat. Suzi's response to that rumor was to notify the Chinese government that the Swiss have decided to add Panda meat to their restaurant offerings unless a 'non-eating' truce is entered into between the respective countries. She's still waiting for a response from Beijing.

This afternoon's events are a given. Suzi will 'ace' her tests and the three of us will stay in downtown Los Angeles so we can eat at the *Pantry* on Ninth and Figueroa, Suzi's favorite non-Chinese restaurant. Bernie will wait outside for us with his friend the newsstand guy until we return with a doggie-bag treat for him... he loves the Pantry's cole slaw
.

Suzi usually wears one of her hats during lunch there because if she didn't, the many customers who walk by and can't seem to resist patting her would wear off all the hair on top of her head. We'll have a pleasant lunch because I make a concerted effort to avoid discussing criminal defense cases with my fascist wife. That way my legal conflicts with her prosecutorial philosophy are kept to a minimum. Suzi usually sits there quietly, relishing the time she can spend with the closest thing she has to a family, and absorbs every word we say. The kid has already expressed her intention to attend Harvard Law School and in a rare expression of generosity, informed Myra that she will always be welcome as an associate in the Suzi B. Law Firm. I like to think that she'll keep me on too.

Back at the boat I see there's a message from the offices of my friend Stuart Schwarzman, the most entrepreneurial person I've ever met. The businesses he's built into successes during the past couple of years are too numerous to list, but the one that stands out most is probably his armored car.

He bought an old one from Brink's Armored Transport and had the words '*He's taking it with him*' painted on the side. Disgruntled heirs hire the truck for up to five hundred bucks a day to have it driven behind the hearse, from the funeral parlor to the cemetery. Stuart's employee Vinnie drives it while wearing a phony uniform, complete with unloaded weapon. The armored car business got so successful that Stuart had to buy a second one, which is now driven by Vinnie's fiancée Olive, who is the subject of the desperate telephone message on my answering machine.

"Mister Sharp, this is Vinnie, and you've got to see us as soon as possible... it's about some surgery for Olive."

This lunatic couple have become like close friends of mine over the past year or so, and the mere mention of surgery sounds very serious, so I immediately return Vinnie's call to see what strange problem they're having this time. Vinnie answers on the first ring, recognizing my number on his caller ID display.

"Oh Mister Sharp... thanks for calling back. How'd Suzi do on her tests today?"

"She did fine, Vin. What's this I hear about Olive having some surgery? Is she okay? Was there an accident of some sort?"

"No, no, Mister Sharp. It's worse than that...she wants to have some surgery done to her face."

Olive is definitely not a raving beauty, but I never noticed anything radically wrong with her face.

"Listen Mister Sharp, we're coming to the boat in a little while because Olive is taking Suzi shopping at the pet store, so I thought if I was there you might be able to spend a little time helping me convince her not to have this surgery done."

"Sure Vinnie. You can tell me about it while they're out shopping, and when they return maybe we can get to the bottom of this."

Vinnie seems relieved, so having at least offered my good deed for the day, I'm now going to sit back and watch the BBC news that they broadcast every weekday afternoon on PBS. I like this international program much better than the local news because they cover all the violence that occurs outside of Southern California. It's really not that different than the local violence, but the BBC has a nice female anchorperson with one of those classy British accents, and that turns me on.

166

It never ceases to amaze me how many countries there are that I've never heard of before, whose main national nesworthiness are civil wars and starving refugees. The most common occupation in those third world countries seems to be 'rebel' or 'insurgent,' and I don't understand what they're always fighting about, because if all the victors want is the 'spoils,' they don't have to waste their time fighting… there seem to be plenty of spoils around in those underdeveloped civilizations. Is having three mud huts that much better than having just one?

Now that the opening 'if it bleeds, it leads' portion of the program is over, we can get to the good stuff. Today's health and fitness report has two topics. First is a report on how much hypochondria costs the world's health systems by those people who always imagine they're sick with something clogging up all the doctors' offices and emergency rooms. If they'd only ask me, I think I have a cure for hypochondria: disease. Maybe they should inject some chronic ailment germ into the arm of each whining hypochondriac… then they'd have something real to take care of, and stop bothering doctors about non-existent ailments.

The second item is about a strain of flu that's spreading around in the United States. This is news to me. The anchor turns to a corres-pondent who tells us about the horrible influenza pandemic that hit this country and the rest of the world back in 1918. From what he says, an estimated 675,000 Americans lost their lives to the flu, which was only a small percentage of the nearly twenty million killed by the disease all over the world in just a few short years. I also learn that a 'pandemic' is defined as an 'epidemic' that goes international.

Modern medicine has really improved, because back then, millions of people died from a sickness that what we now treat with over-the-counter drugs, and also try to avoid by using proper sterile practices in hospitals. Looking for a little more info about this subject on the internet, I learn that the government was operating with the same efficiency then that it does now, as evidenced by the fact that in November of 1918, the

San Francisco health authorities used the air raid sirens to proclaim the end of World War I and let San Franciscans know the flu epidemic was over, and that it was okay for them to celebrate. The citizenry believed the officials, so 30,000 of then went out into the streets for a big party. The very next month, 5,000 new cases of influenza were reported in San Francisco. Nice work, health officials. I guess their descendants were working for the VA seventy-five years later, proclaiming that there is no such thing as bad effects from Agent Orange, and that there's no such thing as Gulf War Syndrome.

I also seem to remember Myra complaining about her trial deputies being required to put in longer days now because of the number of other employees and judges out with the flu. The court calendars are all backed up and they're trying to figure out some way to ease the situation. Thank goodness I'm not involved in that mess downtown. I hate driving down there and back in rush-hour traffic, and the parking situation is especially horrendous because of the big yellow Hummer I ride in. It's not a wussy H-2 or H-3, designed for soccer moms to drive, it's the original 8-foot wide model that the military uses, and one of the first ones released as a domestic model.

Fortunately I don't usually go much farther than the Santa Monica courthouse, because the Uniman Insurance Company assigns some of their smaller west-side auto accident cases to us. After saving old man Uniman from paying out some very large sums on fraudulent insurance claims, he's been showing his appreciation by allowing me to handle some of his less-important auto accident defense cases. The usual procedure is for him to have a case file messengered to the boat, along with an initial retainer fee. My first job on each one is to file an answer to the plaintiff lawyer's lawsuit and then start the civil discovery process by sending out a set of written interrog-atories for the plaintiff to answer under oath. If anything appears interesting in the answer to our 'interrogs,' then we arrange to take depositions of the plaintiff and any others who might be helpful to our defense.

The knocking on our hull must be Vinnie and Olive, and the fact that the dog hasn't even opened one of his eyes indicates that the people who are now stepping up our boarding ladder are 'friendlies,' a category that includes all of our acquaintances and every sworn peace officer who serves west of Sepulveda Boulevard.

Shortly after Vinnie and his fiancée come aboard, Olive, Suzi and Bernie leave on their shopping spree. Vinnie has a concerned look on his face as he sits down with me on the boat's enclosed rear deck.

"Okay Vinnie, what's this surgery stuff all about?"

"Mister Sharp, I don't know why, but Olive wants to get a nose job."

This is a surprise. Olive isn't exactly a cover model, but I never thought her nose was too big. I guess that psychological illnesses like anexoria take a lot of forms. With some people, every time they look at their image in the mirror they see someone who is too fat. Others see someone who definitely needs some bulking up, and others see deformities that need correcting. Olive may be needlessly obsessed with her nose and is seeing a problem that really doesn't exist.

"So what, Vin? If she wants to get a nose job, let her get one. It'll keep her happy, and that important, isn't it?"

"Yeah, sure, but what if that's just the start? I'm afraid that once she gets her nose done, maybe she'll want something else done... where does it end? I want my Olive just the way she is. I've seen some of those complete makeover shows on television and I don't want her turning into something completely different. I like Olive this way. Why does she have to change?"

"I don't know Vin. Do you think there could be some other reason involved? Is she depressed, or going through any other type of changes in her life?"

"Well, you know we're going to set another wedding date soon, but that shouldn't bother her. She's the one who's in a rush for us to get married."

Our conversation gets interrupted a few times by phone calls that come in for Suzi from local police agencies inquiring about some of the crime-fighting software she has installed on her computers. After answering their questions and talking a little more to Vinnie, almost an hour has flown by and I hear paws coming up the boarding ladder.

Suzi and the dog are in their foreward stateroom returning calls to the police, so I take this opportunity to speak to Olive alone while Vinnie relaxes on the aft deck.

"What's going on Olive? Vinnie told me about you wanting to have your nose done. I don't see anything wrong with it. You've got a very nice nose. Is there some medical problem I don't know about? Because lacking that, I don't know why you'd want to do a thing like that."

Every excuse she comes up with seems like it's not the real reason. I guess that a nose job might possibly improve her appearance a little, and that Stuart's insurance will cover all the costs, but I still feel there's something she's not telling me.

"Olive, I know you for a while now, so I'm only going to ask you this question once, and I'd like you to consider something. I've always tried as much as I could to help you and Vinnie out, and you know that I've never lied to you or held anything back. Now I'd like you, as a friend, to give me the same consideration and let me know the real reason why you want to have this elective surgery on your nose."

She thinks about what I've just told her and then starts to slowly explain the real reason.

"Well Mister Sharp, you know we're going to be married soon, and after that we'll probably have kids…"

"Okay, a lot of people do that without getting nose jobs."

"I know, but I'd like to have the surgery before we get married."

"What's the big rush, Olive? You can always have that surgery done. Why do feel it's necessary before you get married?"

"So that my kids won't be born with big noses."

So much for logic. No sense trying to burst her balloon, so I just tell her to make sure she lets the insurance company know her real reason. I'm sure they'll fill her in on the facts of life. They're experts when it comes to turning down requests for medical procedures.

The phone is ringing and it looks very close to Myra's number, so it must be from some other phone in the Criminal Courts Building where her office is located. I answer it and learn that it's Sally Hearn, the presiding judge's clerk.

"Mister Sharp, how are you feeling today?"

"I'm fine Sally, how about yourself?"

"Oh, I'm fine too Mister Sharp. But really, how are you feeling?"

This is a little strange. The only time Sally has ever called me before was to come in and get a court appointment to represent some indigent criminal defendant, and now she's calling to inquire about my health.

"Sally, I assure you that I'm really okay. Is there anything else I can do for you today other than give you a progress report on my health?"

"I'm sorry Mister Sharp, but there's been so much flu going around here lately that we're really concerned about anyone who comes to the courtrooms."

"That's nice Sally, but in case you haven't noticed, I haven't been around there for a while. I'm doing more civil work now, so the criminal courts aren't part of my rounds."

"Yes I know, and that's why Morgan Russell, our new presiding judge, asked me to request that you come down here for an appoint-ment."

"I don't know Sally. I'm really trying to concentrate more on civil matters now, and another criminal case…"

She cuts me off mid-sentence.

"Oh, not to worry Mister Sharp, the judge will see to it that you're not on a criminal case."

"I don't understand what you mean by that Sally. The court doesn't appoint lawyers to represent parties in civil disputes, so what can Judge Russell possibly want me for?

"It's not to represent a party Mister Sharp, you've been selected to act as a temporary judge."

The Final Case
Peter Sharp Legal Mystery #9

Chapter 1

If you don't feel like reading the books, you should at least read the reviews, and that's what I'm doing now. In Los Angeles, if you're not a compulsive shopper, there are very few reasons to buy the New York Sunday Times: One of them is the Book Review Section. Others may include the TV Guide and Sports Section. Some eggheads like the Opinion Section too, but for me it's the Book Reviews and Crossword Puzzle.

It looks like many more women are writing books then in the past. I don't usually take the time to read any books written by women because the way they write, it looks like they care more about what their characters are wearing than what they're doing. Their readers must be those people who watch the Oscars and other award shows just to see what celebrities on the red carpet have on. Who cares which gay dress designer lends a starlet one of his dresses? Don't these women know that they're wearing clothes designed by guys who don't love women? Include me out.

I've been called a lot of things during the past few decades, but 'clothes horse' was never one of them. Being a professional person, I own six suits. Four of them are right off the rack from Sears. They are designated specifically for jury trials, along with the heavy wing-tipped laced shoes, button-down shirts and cheap neckties. I never want to look too slick to a jury.

My other two suits are a different story: they were custom made for me by a Hong Kong tailor who took all my measurements and credit card number over the Internet and made the suits using my request from the sample swatches of material that he sent me. They fit fine, but because my arms are different lengths, this forced me to also order some custom made shirts, so that the requisite ½" of shirtsleeve extends past the end of each coat sleeve.

The shirts are all part of my standard uniform since high school: powder blue button-down. Juries seem to like the button-down look. My custom shirts have white collars with contrasting dark bodies and cost over two hundred bucks each, but what the hell... I'm worth it.

The reason I'm fixating on my wardrobe now is because the Asian Boys are here sorting the laundry, and I happen to notice that they are now folding the ironed items, which include two of my expensive custom shirts. This wouldn't be remarkable except for the fact that I haven't worn either of them for the past month or so.

My past life has just flashed before my eyes and I now see my ex-wife Myra working around our house in Brentwood Glen. She's on the floor painting the baseboard trim in the hall, and she's immaculately attired in one of my most expensive dress shirts, my favorite Cubs baseball cap, a pair of my new navy-blue Jockey shorts, and a pair of my expensive rag socks. If my figures are correct, it means that her painting uniform comes to around two hundred and seventy dollars. What ever happened to those baggy white coveralls that painters used to wear? They probably cost about five dollars each. Not enough for a princess to paint in.

From what I've been told, this type of occurrence is quite common in most households. Women like to lounge around in their husbands' clothes. Kids like to wear their dads' clothes. I wonder how a woman would feel if she came home one evening and found her husband wearing her clothes. On second thought, never mind... here in southern California, nothing is too weird to happen on a regular basis.

It looks like Suzi is no different than Myra. It must be somewhere in every female's genome. They seem to think they've got some God given right to wear our good clothes whenever they want to, like we're sharing a room in some college dorm.

174

There's nothing I could have done to stop it when I was married, and there's no sense even thinking about it now. Things just happen, and this is just one of them.

Another thing that looks like it's inevitable on this boat is that whenever I want to relax and do some reading, Suzi's huge Saint Bernard has already beat me to it and is in my favorite spot on the couch. There's nothing I can do about this either, because no matter what I say or do, he's not moving. Being a huge Saint Bernard, he probably outweighs me by a couple of pounds. I've even tried subterfuge: I went over to the cabinets and shook his box of dog biscuits. Nothing. He knows that Suzi isn't on the boat now, so there's no reason for me to want him to deliver a dog-mail to her. All that the shaking biscuits evoke is his raising of one eyelid in acknowledgment of my futile attempt.

A few minutes later, the only thing that seems to work getting him off the couch takes place. He hears Suzi returning, humming her favorite Chinese melody as she comes up the boarding steps and onto the boat. Bernie jumps off the couch and runs over to the door to greet her. The couch is now mine.

Being the brilliant lawyer that I am, a new plan has just come to me. I leave the boat and walk down the dock to Don Paige's boat. He's our resident technical wizard and we all turn to him for answers to questions about anything involving electricity or computers. My plan is quite simple: Using a DAT recording device, which means **D**igital **A**udio **T**ape to the uninitiated, like I was a before Don explained it to me, we figure out the best way to attach it under the railing of my boat so that its voice-activated controls will turn on automatically and capture any sound made on our boarding steps that's louder than the ambient surroundings.

Hopefully, next time Suzi leaves the boat without the dog, when she returns and hums that tune, the recorder will pick it up and I'll have something to use as a dog-removal device.

It took several days, but things finally lined up properly. Bernie was on the couch and Suzi was down the dock dumping a bag of garbage. When she returned, she hummed, the dog ran to the door to meet her, and I got her on digital audiotape, which is supposed to be almost CD sound quality and if you believe the commercials, as close to the real thing as you can get.

Don fixed the recorder up with a remote control that I can operate inside the boat to turn on the device and play back Suzi humming. It will also reproduce the sound of her footsteps, and the sound level will duplicate the way it is as she comes up the boarding steps. This should fool anyone inside.

Here we go again. Suzi is visiting someone on another boat and Bernie is on the couch. I walk casually over to the window and point my remote control at the recording device. It starts, and we hear Suzi humming her Chinese lullaby. Bernie opens one eyelid in acknowledgement and then closes it again, remaining on the couch. Another good plan goes down the toilet. I guess his hearing isn't as good as I thought it was.

Suzi is home-schooled. At least that's what she's got the Board of Education believing, but I've never seen a teacher come to the boat. Whatever she's doing seems to be working, because the test scores she submitted were so high that the Board now requires her to come downtown to their offices each quarter to take the tests in a monitored setting so they can be sure that there's no hanky panky. She complies, and her grades are still off the charts. The only problem with this is that I have to drive her there because she's not allowed to drive her little e-cart any farther than the Chinese restaurant her mother used to work at down the street on Washington Boulevard.

To make the test-taking trips downtown easier to take, Suzi talks Myra into joining us. After the tests we all go to the Pantry, a restaurant on Ninth and Figueroa, from which Bernie can be brought a side order of their coleslaw to go. On this particular trip, after we drop Myra off at her downtown office, Suzi asks me to stop by the Barnes and Noble bookstore in the marina so she can pick up a book she ordered on fingerprint analysis. Whatever.

The marina Barnes and Noble is just like all other Barnes and Noble bookstores: Big and without soul. It's a typical franchise operation where there is no owner present. I remember one time about ten years ago when Myra and I were still married and we went on a vacation up to northern California. I'm not sure, but I think it was in Sausalito, across from the harbor, where we discovered a delightful, old, three-story bookstore that not only had every book you would ever want to read, but a small sandwich and juice bar on the second floor and plenty of comfortable couches on all three levels.

We wound up spending most of the afternoon there. It was a totally enjoyable experience and we left the store with a shopping bag full of over a couple of hundred dollars worth of books. Give me a privately owned independent bookstore any day of the week. The couches there are more comfortable.

While upstairs in the mystery section of this sterile book establishment I notice a commotion outside in the parking lot. People are lining up down there for some reason. I ask an employee what's going on and am told that the famous author Avery Lawson will be downstairs autographing books. How nice for him to do that. Once again I'm wrong. The clerk informs me that Avery Lawson is a woman. Well, seeing how I feel about female authors, I guess there's no need to go downstairs to have a book autographed, because I have no intention of reading anything that she's written.

Suzi is sitting on a couch reading some book, Bernie is in the car sleeping, and I've already picked out the three or four books I want to buy. An hour or two has passed by and the book signing is over, so I might as well go downstairs and pay for our books. I notice a slender blond female with her back to me. She's packing up some boxes of sales brochures. When she turns around, I'm stunned. This is one of the most beautiful women I've ever seen. I notice that on the table in front of her are some books with their back covers facing up. The photographs on the dust jackets are of her. This must be Avery Lawson. I'm in love. Without even thinking about, I find myself automatically walking over to her.

She looks at me with those big blue eyes and my knees weaken.

"Oh, did you want a book signed?"

No one has ever said that to me before. She's got a beautiful British accent. I clumsily hand her one of the mystery books I've just brought down from upstairs.

"I'm sorry, but I'm only signing books that I've written. Did you buy one?"

She holds up one of her books and I see by the cover that it's one of those dreadful romance novels that women read. The cover features a scantily clad nymphet hanging onto the arm of a muscular guy with long hair whose shirt has been partially ripped off of him. The wind is blowing their hair and his hair looks better than hers. I realize what a fool I've just made of myself and try to recover. I sheepishly grin and try an apology.

"I'm sorry. I've never been to a book signing before. Of course you're only signing your own books. I should have known that. But you should appreciate the fact that being as attractive as you are, someone might want to get your autograph on something other than one of your books."

Boy, that was lame. I think I'd better just turn around and run out of the store before I dig this hole I'm in any deeper. She's now just looking at me and not saying anything, obviously stunned speechless by my stupidity.

"Wait a minute... I've seen you somewhere before... on television on the news. You're an attorney aren't you? Aren't you Peter Sharp?"

Saved. She recognizes me. I'm no longer some schmuck in the bookstore with no identity. I'm now a schmuck with a name.

"Yes, I'm Peter Sharp. I hold a press conference every once in a while, whenever I win a big case."

That's it, the ice is now broken. I may never get another chance, so it's now or never. I see that she's not wearing a wedding ring, so I make my move.

"Listen, I'm sorry about my mistake before. Can I make it up to you with a cup of coffee?"

She doesn't say anything, but seems to be looking past me and down towards the floor. I turn around and see that Suzi has been taking in this entire feeble attempt of mine. Avery looks back at me, and motioning down towards Suzi, asks the sixty-four dollar question.

"A friend of yours?"

"That's debatable. I'm her legal guardian and she's my boss. It's a long story."

"Okay Mister Sharp, you've got my attention. I'll be through here in a little while. Why don't we meet at the Cheesecake Factory in an hour and you can tell me your story. That is, if it's okay with your boss."

On the way back to the boat there is the usual absence of conversation. When I'm ready to leave the boat and walk over to the Cheesecake Factory, Suzi tosses me one of those going-away lines that she's so well known for. The ones that say more than you want them to and leave you no chance to respond. "She's a phony."

An Element of Peril
Peter Sharp Legal Mystery #10

Chapter 1

I am the best telephone pitchman in the world. I know this because I've just made the deal of a lifetime: not to settle a million-dollar personal injury case, not to plea-bargain a murder charge down to trespassing, and not to get 'miss beautiful' to see my etchings. This deal is a true lifesaver: I've talked the Lahaina Yacht Club's bar into stocking a bottle of Patrón Tequila to use for making my margaritas.

I couldn't get them to spring for Patrón's new $500-a-bottle *Burdeos*, but that's okay, because 80-proof Patrón *Silver* will get the job done very nicely.

Now that our little law firm has at least six figures in reserve, I've decided to take a week or so off — and for me, that means relaxation time over in Maui, where I can sit in the Yacht Club and schmooze with other visiting members from all over the world.

When most people hear that I'll be spending some time at my 'yacht club,' they envision luxurious, posh surroundings, complete with butlers who bring your drink and Wall Street Journal to you on a silver platter. Well, if that's what you're looking for, then don't come to the Lahaina Yacht Club, because all we have there at 835 Front Street is a store-front operation with a great kitchen, a great bar, and a great rear balcony that hangs out over the Pacific Ocean, to view the sunset from... and a lot of great members to swap cruising stories with. And while I'm there, I can take some time to relax and mull over what I saw earlier this week that must be ranked as the most amazing things I never thought could be possible: two sightings that completely baffled me.

I travel between my office in Marina del Rey to Beverly Hills once or twice a month to visit a client, and my hopefully traffic-free route includes Overland and Washington Boulevards in Los Angeles and Culver City, respectively.

The first sighting was on Overland, and it happened as I was driving past a Muslim Mosque. Ordinarily, I wouldn't have even looked towards that building, but on this particular day there happened to have been some protest going on, and the combination of a small crowd, plus a few news vans from a local TV station, attracted my attention... and caused me to notice one particular person exiting the Mosque.

When you drive one of the first huge commercialized Hummers, you have to keep your eyes on the road, because whatever you bump into usually gets demolished. Because of this danger, negotiating my beast of a car through a protest area complete with news crews means slowing down and trying not to flatten anything. This task left only a fraction of a second for my glance towards the Mosque entrance, but that brief opportunity shocked me because the person I saw was a perfect double of a close friend and client; someone who I would never believe could be going inside a Mosque. The exiting man and my friend looked exactly the same, with one exception: my friend doesn't wear a cap or have a moustache and short beard.

There are two popular options when being confronted by a situation like this: first, you stare in disbelief, and then follow up by telling everyone you know about what you saw. Second, is to shake your head in disbelief, and tell yourself that what you saw couldn't really be what you think it was, and then go on with your life. I opted for the latter of the two, and didn't think about it again... until the following week.

The second sighting appeared on Washington Boulevard in Culver City, while driving by an attractive building that stands out like a sore thumb in the neighborhood. This is the King Fahd Mosque, and its beautiful architecture draws my attention every time I drive by it... and to my amazement, I see a gentleman entering the Mosque: the same guy I saw last week, leaving the Mosque on Overland.

Fortunately, there was no protest going on, no news crew, and no traffic, so I slowed down a bit and used my new camera-cellphone to snap a picture of the Mosque visitor. I then stopped my Hummer, and using my newly-learned technological expertise, I emailed the photo to my office.

I've heard that everyone has a double: sort of a doppelganger, but not necessarily an evil twin. That statement defies logic because if true, it would mean that out of the approximate six billion people on this earth, half would be exact twins of the other half. I don't think so. However, logic or not, it's always possible that there are people who look amazingly like others. When I was a teenager back in Chicago, attending Von Steuben High School, a lot of the students mistook a friend of mine named Byron for me, and visa versa. We both used to laugh this off. I was especially amused because he was nowhere near as good looking as I was.

I started to drive back to the marina, but my curiosity got the best of me, so I turned the Hummer around and drove back to the Mosque. If that was really my friend going into the Mosque, then his car must be parked nearby, so I drove around, making a two-block radius and finally saw it: a black Lincoln Towncar with the special license plate *JEWBOY*.

There can only be one 'vanity' license plate in the state of California with that name on it, and it is reserved for my Jewish friend Stuart Schwartzman.

To be perfectly fair, the mere fact that his car is parked two blocks away from that Mosque, along with the fact that there are many parking spaces much closer, doesn't mean that the bearded, mustached, hat-wearing doppelganger of my friend Stuart is in that Mosque, but I wouldn't lay odds against it.

Getting back to the office, instead of the immediate series of questions about the mosque picture I emailed earlier I see that it must be 'trim' day, because my efficient little office manager is outside on the dock, using her vacuum-assisted Flowbee to give her Saint Bernard a haircut.

This monthly ritual usually draws a crowd of onlookers who not only enjoy seeing the dog get clipped, but who also line up for a trimming of their own.

Once Suzi finishes with Bernie, she brings out her milk crate, hops up onto it, and the human trimming begins.

You'd be right if you thought that the more upscale boat owners in our area would be a little happier with a professional hair salon, but the group that Suzi works her magic on are the local children, who enjoy having the haircuts done while they hold on to the dog for encouragement.

Shortly after the dog returns to our boat, he approaches me with a message – a note tucked under his collar. Around here, we call that dogmail, because it's Suzi's preferred way of communicating with me. She thinks that email is too impersonal, and that I should have some interaction with a living thing. She's partly right, but I prefer that the living thing be human, female, blonde, and attractive – none of which apply to this beast.

The note is a print of my emailed photo, with a hand-written message: "stick to practicing law." The photo is a blurry shot of my car's steering wheel. So much for evidence of my sightings – and my technical prowess. Now, I'm on my own to find out if what I saw is what I think it was, so I called Jack Bibberman, my investigator. He sounded like his usual jolly self. "What's up boss?"

"Jack, I need you to see someone for me. It's someone you know... here's his address."

"Okay, I recognize the address. What should I see him about?"

"Nothing... just see him, without letting him know you're seeing him."

"Okay, then what?"

"Let me know if his facial appearance is unusual in any way."

I can tell that Jack is a little confused by this assignment, but he's a good soldier: he takes orders and follows instructions without asking any questions. He knows that sooner or later everything will be cleared up for him, and while he's working on this assignment, I can work on some Patrón margaritas while the sun and I both set over the yacht club's ocean balcony.

A Good Alibi
Peter Sharp Legal Mystery #11

Chapter 1

I've never cared much for kids, but from what everyone says, that's because I never had one of my own. The one I have now came to me as a complete package, housebroken, and not needing any particular rearing, and to be perfectly honest, she acts as the sergeant at arms of our modest law firm. I never tell her this, but she's really a good kid most of the time, and does one heck of a job helping out with my cases.
Maybe it's time I do something for her. This being Sunday, I'm taking my weekly exercise walk to the Marina del Rey Liquor store, so on the way back I'll save Suzi some time by stopping to pick up our office mail at the local UPS store. A note left in our box says that they're holding a package for us, but when I ask the clerk for it he refuses to release it to me.

"Excuse me, but it you will please note the name on our box, it says 'Law Offices of Peter Sharp.' And, if you will please note the name and picture on my driver's license, I am that person. I am Peter Sharp, attorney at law, and I would appreciate very much your releasing my package to me."

"I know who you are Mister Sharp, I've seen your picture in the papers... but you're not on the list of persons authorized to pick things up that are delivered here for that box."

"Okay, I give up. Who are the 'persons' authorized to pick things up from my box?"

He looks through his rolodex and gives me three names. "Suzi Braunstein, Jack Bibberman, and Bernie."

"Bernie? Did you say Bernie? What pray tell is this Bernie's last name."

"The Dog. Bernie the Dog."

Great. Three people authorized to pick things up from my box, and *I'm* not one of them. Suzi is, Jack B. is, and even the *dog* is, but I'm not authorized. I press the office's number on my speed-dial, turn on the speakerphone option and hand my cell phone to the clerk. "Here. Please speak to Suzi and get permission to release that package to me."

After four rings, our office phone is picked up and we hear a voicemail message: "Thank you for calling the law offices of Peter Sharp. Due to other commitments, this office will not be accepting any new criminal clients for the next 30 days. Please call back then. Click."

That's it. I've had it with her. Not only has she shut me out of picking up my own mail, but now she's gone ahead and closed the entire business down. I grab my cell phone back from the clerk and start a quick walk back to the boat, hoping she hasn't decided to move it to another slip without telling me.

Good. It's still there. I walk up the boarding steps, enter the pilot house, and find a note attached to the steering wheel.

Peter:
I've gone out on a business errand. Dinner will be served promptly at seven PM this evening.
                              S.B.

Looking out towards the parking lot, I see that her electric cart is gone. She never goes more than a block or two on that thing, so she should be back soon. Nothing to do in the meantime, so I might as well take a little nap. These Saturday walks take a lot out of me. I must have done over a mile.

It's bad enough being woken up from a nap by a noise or someone calling your name, but on this boat, the normal wake-up signal is a gentle nudge of your forehead by something cold and damp – a huge dog's nose. Unfortunately, it will take a minute or two for my senses to get up to speed, so the kid beats me to the conversation.

"You have to buy me a car!"

"What are you talking about? You're only twelve years old. You can't even reach the pedals of a car, let alone drive one legally. You already have that electric cart to go around the neighborhood, and from what I've learned earlier today - that we'll be talking about later, you've even got the dog trained to pick up our mail at the UPS store. What on earth could you possibly need a car for, and why would you expect me to pay for it?"

"I don't expect to drive it. Uncle Jack will drive it for me. Every time we send him out on an assignment I'm always worried that junk he drives will fall apart and he'll get hurt, and not be able to finish up his assignment. And whenever he drives us somewhere, there's no sunroof in his car for Bernie to stick his head up out of.

"And I don't expect you to pay for it. I went to the used car dealer around the corner on Lincoln Boulevard and offered to pay cash out of my own funds for a car, but because I don't have a driver's license, they wouldn't sell me the car. I need you to show them your license so that you can buy the car for me."

"Well, I'd like to help you out kiddo, but according to the voicemail message I got from your answering machine this afternoon when I wasn't allowed to pick up my own mail, I am currently out of business, so I don't feel like buying a car. Do you have any good reason for shutting us down for the next few weeks?"

"Yes Peter. There's a case I don't want you to take, because it would conflict with something else I'm now working on. And, if you'll trust me on this one, you may wind up with a nice fee for doing very little."

Okay. She's got an answer for everything, and doing very little is my specialty. As I rinse off my forehead they disappear below into their private enclave in our yacht's foreward stateroom. Boy, do I pity any poor guy with a young daughter who has to actually raise her from scratch. This one's got plenty of her own money from previous settlements of suits that caused the death of her mother and stepfather, and she's a computer genius, but she's still a handful.

I've got some time to kill before dinner, so perhaps now will be a good time to do the Sunday crossword puzzle. The newspaper is on the table, but when going through the section where the crossword puzzle usually is, I can't find it.

I hate when this happens. Whenever those idiots decide to start putting the puzzle in another section, it forces me to go through every page of every section, looking for it.

No luck. I've gone through every page of this huge Sunday paper. Wait a minute. In the section it usually appears, there seems to be a page missing. I can't believe she'd purposely tear out a page to stop me from doing the puzzle. Looking closer, I notice that it's not just the puzzle that's gone – it's the entire four-page fold that the puzzle was on. She must have wanted to keep something that was printed there – probably an article that has something to do with why she closed us down for the month and told me to 'trust her.' No problem, I'll just call my friend Stuart and have him save those pages for me out of his paper. I'm curious to know what caught her interest, and it's been a while since I spent some time with Stuart, so I might as well drive over to his place.

Stuart Schwarzman is an old friend and client, and he is the most entrepreneurial person I've ever met. He has a commercial compound in the San Fernando Valley that consists of a large concrete tilt-up warehouse-type building that includes some windowed storefronts facing the street. Some of the many businesses he runs out of his place include the tattoo-removal parlor, a pawn shop, his private investigation business, a used car operation that sells recovered stolen vehicles he buys from some insurance company's dealer in New Jersey, and various other ventures.

He's out in front of his place waiting as I pull up, and as usual, he's all excited about his latest business idea. As soon as he gets into my Hummer and hands me the newspaper pages I asked him about, he starts in.

"Peter, I finally figured out how to make money without working. I'm going into the equipment rental business. Oh, by the way, do you mind riding by the police station? I want to drop something off there."

Okay, that sounds pretty normal for him. I really don't have to say anything to learn more, because if I know Stuart, he'll jump on the few seconds of silence as a request for more information.

"I know that sounds strange to you Peter, but this package I've got in my hand explains it all... and that's why I'm dropping it off for the cops to look it over. Do you know what BADCAT means?

"I didn't think you did. it's an acronym for a special police unit they've got going. It stands for Burglary Auto Division, Commercial Auto Thefts. And that's who I'll be doing business with."

"All right Stuart, you've done it again. I'm hooked. What is this new business deal you've got going?"

"If you watch those police shows like I do, then you'll know what a *bait car* is. That's what the cops use to catch auto thieves. They have a specially rigged car equipped with GPS that has hidden cameras inside, and with remote controlled door locks and a kill switch. They'll park the thing in an area with a high auto theft rate, and wait for someone to come along and steal it.

"Once the crooks are inside the car, the police command center tracks it using the GPS sending device, and when the chase cars are ready to make an arrest, the command center locks the doors, trapping the crooks inside, and then kills the engine.

"When the crooks discover they're locked in the car and hear the police issuing instructions to them on a loud speaker, they know it's over for them, and they usually follow instructions and surrender without any resistance."

"Yeah, I've seen those things on television, Stu, but how do you fit into that picture?"

"Ah, there's the rub, Peter. Not every police department has the budget to buy and equip bait cars, set up a command center, and do all the rest that it takes to get the bait car program up and running... and that's where I come in.

"Remember my used car business? The one I have that sells those stolen and recovered Toyota Camrys I have trucked in from New Jersey? Well according to national statistics, the Camry is one of the most popular theft items, along with the Hondas. What I do is install the camera and some other little trick items, and rent the car out to police departments."

"What about a command center? Who does the tracking, the door locking and the engine killing? Are you intending to do all of that for the police?"

"No need to, Peter. That's what makes my operation so attractive. We accomplish the same thing on a budget. First of all, we don't have GPS units. Instead, we have a hidden cell phone strapped under the car that is automatically turned on when the engine starts. With today's technology, any cell phone that's turned on can be tracked by triangulating the cells it can receive signals from. Besides, the bait car will be under surveillance at all times by an undercover BADCAT unit.

"And there's no need for a command center, because the door locks are also connected to the ignition system, so they silently and automatically lock when the engine starts. And for a kill switch, we rigged up a portable system with a range of about two hundred feet, so the undercover unit can kill the engine from almost a half block away."

"That might work Stu, but what happens if they lose sight of the bait car or get separated from it in traffic. By the time they triangulate and find it ten minutes later, there's no telling where it might be. And if the engine's turned off while the car's hiding in a garage, they'll never be able to find it."

"Not to worry, my friend. First of all, there's a governor on the speed control, so the car can't do more than forty. And as far as distance is concerned, the car's fuel indicator shows a full tank, but there's really only about a gallon of gas in the car, so it can't go more that about fifteen to twenty miles before dying on its own. And, if the car engine stops for lack of gas instead of being intentionally killed by a chase car, the burglar alarm goes off, to make it easier to find. It's a complete economy bait car, perfect for small police departments who only want to pay five hundred bucks per rental period.

"The money they save on command center personnel and electronics more than pays for the rental, and the cost can be added to the perps' conditions of probation and/or parole. It's a win-win deal, and I've already got a bunch of local departments interested in using it."

As I drive back to the marina, I can't stop thinking what a business genius Stuart is. The only thing taking my mind off of Stuart is the dinner that will be waiting for me on the boat, because Suzi will be doing her thing. She's too short to use the boat's cooking appliances, but she doesn't have to. Her late mother was the manager of a Szechwan restaurant around the corner on Washington Boulevard, and four of the young guys who work there have formed a group that we've nicknamed 'the Asian Boys.' In addition to their services as food delivery and catering set-up, they also have learned how to do really good varnishing, so they are quite popular here in the marina.

I'm sure that Suzi will be having them bring over something really good tonight, so when she says "dinner will be at seven," I know that it will be served promptly at that time, and I'll be sitting at the table with a fork in one hand, waiting for my plate. The kid has already given up on trying to teach me how to use chopsticks."

While waiting to take my place at the dinner table, I glance over the pages that Stuart gave me... the ones that were missing from our Sunday paper. The crossword puzzle is here, so my after-dinner relaxation is guaranteed. The only other things I notice are some articles about a recent unsolved murder case the District Attorney is looking into.

This isn't surprising. My ex-wife Myra is the District Attorney, and has really bonded with Suzi, who would like nothing more than to see the two of us back together again making a complete family for her. She probably has a scrap book somewhere and keeps clippings about her friend Myra.

Reading through the article, it looks like they don't have much to go on. The lady killed was someone named Gussie, who was taking care of her backyard gardening when someone bopped her quite hard on the head, when into her house, and left with about two hundred in cash.

Dinner is served, and it's delicious as usual. The only guests we have this evening are Jack Bibberman, the best investigator in town, and Laverne, a lady who lives on one of the small houseboats that our anchorage rents out. Jack is probably here because he's meeting with Suzi about an assignment she'll no doubt be giving him, and Laverne's here because I want to stay on her good side because she's the only alternative I have this month to the *Happy Ending Massage Parlor* a mile away in Venice.

There's not very much conversation during dinner, except for everyone telling me how nice it would be if I would sign the papers so Suzi could by the used car she wants from the used car dealer around the corner on Lincoln Avenue. I'm putting up a pretty good argument for not signing the papers.

Legally Dead
Peter Sharp Legal Mystery #12

Chapter 1

Local news sucks. I hate the way they always make it look like a crime report, with the worst things that people do to each other always being the lead stories.

Strangely enough though, today they finally opened with an item that didn't depress me. It was about a killer who killed another killer... and got caught in the act.

Local news sucks. I hate the way they always make it look like a crime report, with the worst things that people do to each other always being the lead
The news producers realize that nothing's as boring as a talking head in a studio, so they always try to include some stock footage or place their reporter outside of an empty building where something in the story took place. They also like to do interviews of anyone who they feel can add some irrelevant information to the story, like neighbors of a serial killer who are shocked to learn about their living in such close proximity to the lunatic, but thought that he was always a 'nice, quiet person, who always kept to himself.'

Today's news about the killer gives the reporter a chance to pose on the steps of the downtown Criminal Courts Building, and whenever there's a news camera crew there, my ex-wife Myra, the District Attorney usually makes sure to appear on the scene just in time to be interviewed... and today is no different. This popular event brings her two biggest fans out of the foreward stateroom to watch the big screen in our boat's main salon.

The dog barks hello as Myra is introduced while Suzi sits on the floor watching. Myra is in her usual good public form as she saves the reporter any inconvenience caused by actually being required to ask questions. Myra likes to maintain control of any relationship she's in, even if it's only a brief one with a reporter. Her statement is a brief one:

"Earlier today, our office filed charges against John 'the bat' Zellini, for one count of violating section 187 of the California Penal Code... murder in the first degree.

"The defendant was not aware of the fact that at the time of the crime, his victim was under surveillance by a special police unit in our organized crime task force, and the entire event was captured on videotape."

The reporters start shouting out questions to Myra. She pretends to listen to a few of them and then continues, feeling confident that whatever she says will surely answer any questions they might have – even if they're not smart enough to ask them.

"In answer to your questions, the victim was a reputed member of a criminal organization that was trying to establish itself locally in the garbage collection business. We have information that leads us to believe that there seems to have been a 'turf' war starting up, concerning certain apartment-building areas of the city that require commercial trash vehicles to empty their dumpsters daily.

"These garbage disposal contracts are quite profitable, and it appears that less-than legitimate groups fight over them like the crack dealers fight over which street corner to deal from.

"Another issue to be considered is if this was a murder-for-hire and if so, would we be seeking the death penalty for the special circumstances involved in a crime of this nature. We are still investigating that aspect of the incident and the punishment sought will depend a great deal on whether or not we get any cooperation from the defendant.

"He has been taken to a special location for his own protection, and will be brought to court for arraignment next week. At that time, we will make a further statement to update you."

That being said, the interview ends, the reporter wraps up her piece with the courthouse appearing in the background, and the dynamic duo exits my salon – and I've learned that Myra actually put into place that special top-secret police unit she always told me they should have. The way she used to talk about it, the unit would keep their eye on the most suspicious criminals in the jurisdiction – the ones with extensive criminal records who could be depended upon to continue their criminal enterprises.

Myra has combined her crime-fighting instincts with her business skills, because by using utilizing the RICO laws that apply only to those **R**acketeer **I**nfluenced **C**orrupt **O**rganizations, her department is allowed to legally seize assets of criminals that were purchased with funds illegally gained… and I believe that in most cases the seizing departments are permitted to keep a large percentage of the take, to be used in furtherance of fighting crime. I'm sure any matter that can be a RICO case takes a high priority in her office, and I wouldn't be surprised if that's why her special surveillance unit was concentrating on this particular victim.

Now that I've seen what will probably be the only non-depressing local news item of this year, I switch the channel over to cable, where I can alternately surf between Keith Olbermann on MSNBC and Bill O'Reilly on Fox News. In our neighborhood both of those satellite shows are on during the same time period from five to six PM. They've been having a bitter feud for the past few years that has been giving them both quite a bit of coverage, especially in the blogosphere, and I have a hunch that they cooked it up between them as a publicity stunt.

The cable shows don't mention our local murder, but I'm sure that the killer-kills-killer angle is too good a 'hook' for the networks to ignore, so it'll surely to pop up here and there on the small screen and the internet.

Suzi's mother used to be the manager at a Szechwan restaurant around the corner on Washington Boulevard, and four of their busboy/waiters have formed a crew that takes on varnishing and other minor maintenance jobs for the boat owners in our marina. They've acquired the nickname of the 'Asian Boys,' and because their leader appears to be none other than my office-manager/boatmate Suzi, the boys will be bringing a gourmet dinner to the boat this evening, where the dynamic duo and I will be joined by my friend and client Stuart Schwartzman, plus whatever other guests Suzi has invited tonight for our usual seven PM seating.

Our anchorage rents out some small houseboats for liveaboards, and one of them is on our dock. It's occupied by an approximately 40-ish redheaded female who I have had an opportunity to *know*, in a biblical sense. I have no idea what she does for a living, but a husky man picks her up every morning and brings her home every evening. I guess it's just some guy at work she car-pools with, but I never really cared enough to inquire about it.

Tonight's dinner will be an anniversary of our buying this 50-foot trawler yacht we operate on, so Suzi's invited some extra guests to dinner. Laverne will be here, as will Victor, Jack B., and Stuart. Myra was invited too, but she declined, due to an excessive caseload she's burdened with due to some recent spate of bad guys getting arrested for various crimes.

When Suzi learned that Myra wouldn't be coming she allowed me to invite Laverne. Suzi doesn't want the two of them around me at the same time because she's still working on her master plan to get me back together with Myra, so that she can have a complete set of parents.

Now that Laverne will be coming, Suzi has instructed the Asian Boys to stop at the liquor store to pick up a box of Laverne's favorite wine.

Stuart usually arrives a little early so that he can tell me about whatever new business venture he's involved in this week. He's gotta be the most entrepreneurial guy I've ever met. But to my surprise, he hasn't started anything new this month, instead, he's brought a friend of his along for dinner – Maury, a gentleman who Stuart introduced me to several years ago.

Maury was a professional musician for many years and accepted an invitation to join the symphony orchestra in Bogotá, Colombia. He's now back in our country making his annual visit to friends and family, so Suzi asked Stuart to bring him along for dinner this evening.

In between courses, Maury tells us some interesting stories about life in Colombia, and how the drug traffic affects his community. From what he explains, the drug kingpins are revered in the community.
Notwithstanding the fact that they wouldn't hesitate one second to have you killed if you interfered in any way with their business, they are very generous, contributing to local charities and being involved as supporters of the arts, which includes the symphony orchestra Maury performs with.

When Maury flies between Colombia and California he changes planes in Florida and manages to pick up some Cuban cigars. Suzi doesn't allow smoking in the boat, which is okay, because I'm not a smoker – but once in a while I like to enjoy a good Cuban cigar on the aft deck, and tonight is the perfect opportunity for that, so the three of us guys make our way out to the chaise lounges waiting for us, where we'll be spending the next hour puffing away and watching the summer sun set over the Pacific Ocean.

After a few of Maury's interesting tidbits, Stuart tells us about an idea he's been tinkering with for the past few years that now might be a

198

distinct possibility. Unlike his other numerous enterprises, this one will be devoted to raising significant amounts of money for various charities. It involves the use of a recently-closed restaurant to host dinners where large round tables will be used to seat one major celebrity guest plus eleven wealthy donors who are willing to pay twenty-five-hundred-dollars per seat to have dinner with the celeb.

As Stuart continues with his business idea, I see that the kid is in the main salon watching some news show on our big flat plasma screen. The thing that really catches my eye is an interview being conducted, because once again my ex-wife District Attorney Myra Scot Sharp is being interviewed. We put our Havanas down and go inside to see what else Myra has to say this evening. This additional appearance was brought about by the naming of an attorney to represent the killer that Myra talked about in her earlier interview.

By the time we all get into place by the television screen, Myra's part of the interview is over, but we hear the reporter summing up her interview: "As the District Attorney has just stated, the defendant John Zellini, now formally charged with first-degree murder, has requested that the court replace his public defender with a respected member of the local criminal defense bar, a private attorney.

"The District Attorney voiced no objection to this request, and the court has agreed to the defendant's wishes. The reason that we've made this interruption of your normal evening programming is because that private criminal defense attorney's office has been notified and has agreed to the court appointment, and it happens to be none other than District Attorney Myra Scot Sharp's former husband – attorney Peter Sharp!"

How to Rob a Bank
Peter Sharp Legal Mystery #13

Chapter 1

I've been out of town for the past couple of weeks, hanging out at the Lahaina Yacht Club in Maui. As with all other members, they've put an updated picture of my boat, complete with the LYC flag flying on the bow in the most recent club mailing, and because it's a nice 50-foot Grand Banks trawler yacht, members of the club seem to have the mistaken opinion that I actually know how to start the engines and drive the darn thing.

With my new-found yachting reputation, I seem to be getting a little more respect here at the club, and since the bar has finally acceded to my pleas and they now stock Patròn Tequila, I believe the margaritas taste much better - notwithstanding the fact that they cost a little more than ones made with the stuff they pour from that mysterious 'well' behind every commercial bar.

Ever since reading Jacques Futrelle's *The Problem in Cell 13*, I've been hooked on 'locked-room' mysteries, and this situation with Brodini the magician has certainly attracted not only my attention, but also that of most thinking people who watch television.

A little while ago I was involved in another locked-room mystery that took place in the steel-encased panic room of a paranoid rich guy who lived out here on the Peninsula, an exclusive ocean-side neighborhood that adjoins Marina del Rey California, where my yacht is parked - and from where I operate my small law firm, assisted by little Suzi, a 12-½ adorable Chinese computer genius who I let help me out with solutions to my criminal cases. But this one seems a little more intense than the last one, because here we have a witness who saw the defendant enter the vault, and many other witnesses who watched the defendant commit what looked like crimes on the vault's camera monitors.

The fact that the supposed defendant was nowhere to be found when the authorities entered the bank's vault have no bearing on the matter, other than to raise the question of how he escaped. Legally speaking, either a crime was committed or it wasn't: the defendant's escape or non-escape doesn't erase the fact that a crime may have taken place. All I can say at this point is that the plane ride back to LAX is a pleasant one, and I'm glad I'm not involved in this vault mess. As the matter stands, here's everything I've heard about the case, and it's about the same amount that everyone else in the world knows, with the exception of the Great Brodini. This is an excerpt from a local news reporter's article. She happened to have been on the scene at the time these events took place and also interviewed persons present to prepare her article.

The Great Bank Robbery:
The Great Brodini is a creature of habit. He gets up at the same time each day, calls the Scharf Limousine Company for a Lincoln Town Car to be sent to his condo building, and after dressing impeccably is driven to his office, or wherever else his career requires that he appear.

On this particular day, Scharf's best driver, Raul Wainer, pulled into the Beverly Hills Wilshire Boulevard underground parking garage beneath Brodini's luxurious condo complex at 8:45 AM, called his client to let him know he was waiting near the elevator, and several minutes later took the magician on a 15-minute drive to the Marina del Rey branch of Myerson Savings & Loan... one of the few lending institutions that is still financially healthy, because it avoided getting involved in the sub-prime lending mess. Jules Beider, the bank's CEO, just *didn't understand* the *new* way that real estate finance worked: He couldn't figure out how to make a profit by making low-interest adjustable-rate mortgage loans to people with no down-payment and no substantial reliable income or other means of making payments when he loans would re-set with new higher rates, on the inflated and over-priced property that they just were not qualified to purchase... but he knows of many other banks that *did understand* how things worked – and he's now entering into negotiations to buy one or two of them at their bankruptcy sales.

- - - - - -

Brodini goes to this bank several times a month for two reasons: first, he wants to visit his safe-deposit box to either pick up or drop off plans for an illusion he's working on or updates to the book he's in the process of writing – and secondly, to drop in at Rottman's Haberdashery next door to the bank, where he will purchase a new silk tie to wear later that day during whatever luncheon he's been invited to.

Due to his celebrity status as a popular nightclub act in Las Vegas and many west coast venues, Brodini is afforded some perks, in an attempt to avoid awkward situations that usually crop up whenever people of his fame are thrust in the general populace. One of those perks is being allowed to enter the bank at 9:00 in the morning, when Bryce Chalem the manager opens the front door to go in.

At first the bank was reluctant to grant this privilege to the magician, but Chalem and Beider finally came to the conclusion that it would be better to let Brodini conduct his safe-deposit business well before the bank's employees and general public were present. Their thinking was that the fewer disturb-ances during business hours, the better.

Thanks to this perk, Wainer was allowed to park the Town Car right in front of the Bank. As usual, their timing was perfect, because just as Brodini got out of the car, he met the manager opening the front door. They both went inside together and Chalem then locked the door behind them, not planning to open it again until 9:30, when the bank's employees would be arriving for the day's work, and also to allow Brodini to exit.

While Wainer waited outside the bank, he sat there grumbling to himself about what he considered to be terrible landscaping around the building. The only reason that Scharf kept him on is because of the well-known secret that Raul always carried a small loaded gun – and Brodini, who was aware of this, enjoyed the additional security. When Wainer wasn't driving, he was exercising his gambling habit, and felt better being armed after frequent large Texas Hold'em winnings at private card games.

Inside the bank, Chalem went to his desk, removed some keys from a drawer, and then changed into his Myerson blazer, a bright green hopsack item bearing the Myerson crest - a required garment for all bank officers. Myerson's founding partner, Jules Beider's father, was a stickler for formality and his son kept the tradition going. Fancy dressing was always a family trait, and both Beider's wife, and his Cuban mistress appreciated their separate times being out with the generous, big-spending, well-dressed businessman. He loved to spend money on his women.

Chalem and Brodini walked to the rear of the bank, where Chalem used his key to open a lock and slide open a steel gate, a security measure about ten feet from the vault entrance. The time-lock on the vault door allowed it to be opened at 9:10 AM, and when the large thick door was swung open, the manager and the magician both walked into the vault.

Once inside the small 7-foot wide by 20-foot long room, Chalem used another bank key and along with Brodini's key, they opened up the small locked cabinet door behind which was the magician's safe-deposit box. At this time, Brodini made a strange request. "Bryce, I don't think I'll be going into one of the small rooms outside the vault this morning, so if it's okay with you, I'll just stay in here and do my box business. I'll call for you in a while, when it's time for you to come in and lock the box compartment."

The manager agreed and Brodini was grateful. So grateful in fact, that he put his arm around Chalem and thanked him for his cooperation over the many months that the box was being used. As the manager was leaving the vault, Brodini shook his hand vigorously and made one other request: "Oh, by the way, since I'll be staying here in the vault for another few minutes or so, would you please slide the metal gate closed on your way out? I'd rather not have any early-arriving bank employee wander in here while my box is open and some of my magic trick blueprints are out in the open."

Chalem didn't mind this second request either, and after leaving the vault, he slammed closed the security gate behind him as he entered the main bank lobby. It locked automatically.

About 20 minutes later, the bank's security guard was let in the front door, and when he went to his station and turned on the small set of monitors, one of them caught his attention and he called Chalem over to look at it. It was the vault camera, and to their amazement there was a beautiful, clear view of Brodini holding a ring of keys, and systematically opening one safe-deposit box after another and emptying their contents into a large sack.

Chalem excitedly told the guard to call the police, as he hit the alarm button that automatically notifies the authorities and the FBI, who also investigate crimes against federally chartered institutions. He then rushed to the sliding metal gate, and when reaching into his pocket for the key, he discovered that it was missing. In its place was a small computer-printed note:

> *Bryce:*
> *Sorry to inconvenience you for a while, but I've got some things to do here in the vault this morning.*
> *Brodini*

Chalem then realized that Brodini had picked his pocket earlier, and that now everyone was locked out of the vault until they could get the security gate open again. Towards that end, Chalem called Beider, who tried to get him to relax. "Bryce, take it easy. Brodini may be up to some shenanigans in the vault, but where's he gonna go? He's in the vault now, and the steel gate behind him is locked. Even if he's got the key, when he tries to unlock it to leave, you'll have a whole squad of police and FBI guys waiting for him. We can't lose with this: there'll be no loss of client assets, and the publicity of us foiling a robbery attempt will enhance our security capability in the mind of the public. It's a win-win for all of us."

The vault camera's image was put up on the large screen monitors placed in various strategic locations around the bank lobby, and the bank employees, police, and FBI were all entertained for while, waiting for the locksmith's crew to arrive and open up the sliding metal gate. The one thing on everyone's mind was 'what the heck is he thinking?' They couldn't figure out why Brodini would risk his career and his freedom with such a dumb stunt. There would be no getting away, no profit from the theft, and nothing left of his career... absolutely no upside. He's got nothing to gain and everything to lose.

It took about a half hour before the vault company's locksmith crew arrived, and then another half hour for them to use welding torches to break through the metal security gate's lock. When they finally got the metal gate open, the law enforcement people used a bullhorn to communicate with Brodini. "Mister Brodini, this is special agent Wilkinson, with the FBI. We don't want any problems here, and certainly don't want you to be hurt in any way, so please pick up the telephone in the vault so we can discuss your safely coming out of the vault. I'm sure you know there's no getting away from here, so please, let's do it the easy way. No one will be hurt, and we can all leave here safely."

Silence. No response from inside the vault. Everyone looked over towards Chalem, who was sitting behind his desk with the private vault phone extension to his ear. He looked toward the cops and nodded from left to right, indicating that Brodini hadn't picked up the vault phone.

The law enforcement contingent decided that they would rather not rush

Writing Mystery Novels   Grossman

into the vault. Instead they made arrangements to fire a tear gas grenade into the vault and force Brodini out to them. To avoid the gas affecting people outside the vault, they set up some fans blowing towards the vault door, to keep the gas vapors concentrated inside the vault. As a last result, they tried to coax Brodini out again with the bullhorn. "Mister Brodini, this is special agent Wilkinson. If you don't come out of there with your hands in the air, in about 30 seconds we're going to be firing a tear gas grenade into the vault. I suggest that if you decide to stay in there for a while that you get as close to the ajar vault door so that you won't be injured with the gas grenade is fired in there."

Still no response. They looked over to Chalem, and once again he nodded in the negative that the vault phone wasn't being used.

Bang! The rifle was fired and the grenade flew into the vault. The fans were turned on blowing towards the vault, and even though a small amount of gas seeped out, no one outside the vault was affected by it. The SWAT leader motioned to his crew, and completely covered in their armored uniforms with gas masks on, five of them rushed into the bank vault, guns drawn. A second or two later, we heard the SWAT team's leader tell the sergeant in the lobby the word that stunned everyone, as it was broadcast on his walky-talky: "Clear!"

Everyone there exchanged looks of amazement as the five SWAT officers came back out of the vault, removing their gas masks and holstering their weapons. They told their sergeant that the bank vault was empty. Brodini was gone. There was no one in there.

That was the end of her article

Closing Comments

It's never been a very good idea to allow people to have the access to contact celebrities directly. If you want to get a message to George Clooney, you're going to have to send it through his fan club website (where he'll probably never see it), or through his publicist or agent (where he'll definitely never see it).

My philosophy is that readers are a little different. They're not usually the crazed stalker-type of fans who will either want to sneak into your house at night and steal your underwear, think that you're in love with them, or want to do you harm. That's why I experimented in my books by giving my readers an opportunity to communicate with me – I gave them an email address my publisher provided for me.

Magic Lamp Press screens the emails to weed out any wackos (none have appeared yet, so you can be the first, if you want to) and then forwards the messages to me... and I do my best to answer each one of them.

The only time I've ever seen this done before is by the two Steves (Dubner and Leavitt) who wrote **_Freako-nomics_**. I sent them an email about a method I used to save money when using a real estate broker, and they responded quite warmly, so
I decided to use their courteous method and added a couple of slight twists:

First, I bought some Avery self-adhesive labels at Staples (2 to a page) and designed an 'autograph' plate that has a space for a person's name, thanks them for obtaining the book, urges them to read more of my books, and has some space for me to affix my autograph, using a blue Sharpie pen;
[For eBook customers, I offer to send a personalized thank-you letter]

Second, I gave out the email address of **editor@MagicLampPress.com** where I could be reached;

Third, I offered to send any requesting reader an autographed stick-on plate that they could put inside the front cover of the book (plus one of my bookmarks), to show that they actually know the author;

Fourth, I invited them to comment on any blatant typographical errors they may have found. This turned every reader into an assistant proof-reader.

Book sales have been increasing every month, and to be quite honest, I don't know what the main cause of that is. As mentioned, I've done everything I could think of to help with the marketing, so to make myself feel good, I'm just telling myself that the reason sales are on the upswing is because the books are that good and people like them. Who knows? That might even be the reason.

As for the feedback from readers, I heard from a lady in Texas who read all of the books and sent me pages of typo corrections to make. Typos are like cockroaches, alligators and politicians named Clinton or Bush: you can never completely get rid of them. The major publishing houses must have hundreds of people chained to tables in their basements, looking for typos to correct before printing thousands of copies of a book, but as you may have noticed occasionally one or two get through anyway.

We don't have basements under the houses in California, so proofreaders are in short supply, and I must confess that the lady from Texas did a great job. After all of her corrections were made (for which I thanked her profusely), I haven't had one complaint about typos from a reader. The truly amazing thing about her finding so many of them was because the books had been proof-read by several others previously.

I have a friend who is a voracious reader, as are his wife and two children, so I made a deal with them: I would give them a book to read and pay them $50 for a reading fee, plus $1 for each typo they would find.

First, the father would read it, marking each error he found. Then the book would be given to the mother, who would do the same, and then the daughter and lastly the son. They each used a different colored marking pen, and at the end they would count the errors found by each as sort of an inter-family competition.

It is tremendously helpful for a writer to have two important skills, both of which I am fortunate to possess: 1. being a speed typist, and 2. being full of bull____.

The good thing about skill number 1 is that anything you want to say can get through the keyboard and onto the page quickly. The bad thing is that the faster you type, the more errors you make (at least I do)... and if there's one thing I hate to do is proof-read my own stuff, because I wind up re-writing everything and then the book never gets done, but it's something that absolutely must be done. All that a proof-reader can do is correct typos, but a good editor (that's you, if you aren't with a big publishing house) can also correct intentions of the characters and improve plot points.

As for skill number 2... well, either you're full of it, or you're not. If you're curious about that, just ask your closest friends.

___

Thank you very much for reading this book. I hope that someday soon when someone asks if you've read a good book lately, you'll be able to say the same thing I usually say: "Not really, I'm too busy writing another one of my own."

Gene Grossman

Editor's note:

If you've purchased this print version, you may subsequently learn that a book of the same title has been offered as an eBook at various websites, for as little as $2.95

It is not the same as this one. It is by the same author, and addresses the same subject matter, but the low-cost eBook version is an abbreviated one (less than third the number of pages as this) and does not contain the same amount of information as this printed one (no sample chapters, not as much technical stuff, etc., etc.)... and, you now actually own this one and can refer to it in perpetuity – it's not sitting on someone else's server.

Magic Lamp Press

P.S.

If you'd like to receive a free bookmark, please drop us a line to **editor@MagicLampPress** with a request, along with any other comments you may have about the subject, typos, the books, or anything else on your mind – and, if you sincerely say you liked this book, you might even get a response from one of our editors (or maybe even from Gene, if he's in town in-between book signings).

Printed in Great Britain
by Amazon.co.uk, Ltd.,
Marston Gate.